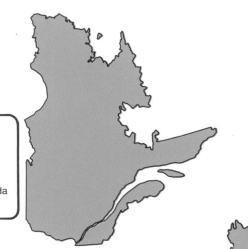

Quebec

Entry into Confederation:	July 1, 1867
Capital:	Quebec City
Area: Land	1 356 790 km²
Water	183 890 km²
Total area	1 540 680 km² 15.5% of Canada
Highest point of land:	Mont d'Iberville 1 622 m

Newfoundland

Entry into Confederation:	March 31, 1949
Capital:	St. John's
Area: Land	371 690 km²
Water	34 030 km²
Total area	405 720 km² 4.1% of Canada
Highest point of land:	Mount Caubvick 1 622 m

Prince Edward Island

Entry into Confederation:	July 1, 1873
Capital:	Charlottetown
Area: Land	5 660 km²
Water	—
Total area	5 660 km² 0.1% of Canada
Highest point of land:	Queen's County 142 m

Nova Scotia

Entry into Confederation:	July 1, 1867
Capital:	Halifax
Area: Land	52 840 km²
Water	2 650 km²
Total area	55 490 km² 0.6% of Canada
Highest point of land:	Cape Breton Highlands 532 m

New Brunswick

Entry into Confederation:	July 1, 1867
Capital:	Fredericton
Area: Land	72 090 km²
Water	1 350 km²
Total area	73 440 km² 0.7% of Canada
Highest point of land:	Mount Carleton 820 m

D1266068

Ontario

Entry into Confederation:	July 1, 1867
Capital:	Toronto
Area: Land	891 190 km²
Water	177 390 km²
Total area	1 068 580 km² 10.7% of Canada
Highest point of land:	Ishpatina Ridge 693 m

Canada

Total land area	9 215 430
Inland water	755 180
Total	9 970 610

SOURCES: The Canadian Encyclopedia Jr. *Hurtig*
The Canadian World Almanac 1991 *Global Press*

The Macmillan School Atlas

Third Edition

Ronald C. Daly

 EDUCATIONAL PUBLISHING COMPANY
A DIVISION OF CANADA PUBLISHING CORPORATION
TORONTO ONTARIO CANADA

Canadian Cataloguing in Publication Data

Daly, Ronald C., 1932–
  The Macmillan school atlas

3rd ed.
Includes index.
ISBN 0-7715-8269-2

1. Atlases, Canadian. I. Waller, John R. II. Title.

G1021.D35 1991   912   C91-094642-6

Text Design and Illustrations: Full Spectrum Art

Maps : All maps by John Waller, except pages 96-97,
    106-107, 121, 122-123 by Joe Stevens

Cover Photo: Masahiro Sano, Masterfile

Cover Design: Susan Weiss

Editorial Team: Anne Marie Moro, Carol Waldock, Carolyn
    Leaver, Tilly Crawley

ISBN 0-7715-**8269-2**

6 7 8 9 10 FP 99 98 97 96 95

Written, Printed, and Bound in Canada

Acknowledgments

p. 1 The British Library; p. 2 NASA; p. 6, 26 National Air Photo Library/Energy, Mines and Resources Canada; p. 18 left, p. 18 middle, p. 24 top, p. 24 middle, p. 24 bottom left, p. 37 (Quebec), p. 39 top left, p. 39 top right, p. 43 top right Robert Waldock; p. 18 (illustration) Anne Stanley; p. 18 right, p. 19 middle Jennifer Walti-Walters; p. 19 left, p. 37 (Regina) S.P.M.C.—Photographic Services Agency; p. 19 right, p. 43 bottom left Province of British Columbia; p. 20 top Tokyo Stock Exchange, Tokyo, Japan; p. 21 top Dilip Mehta © ACDI/CIDA; p. 20 bottom Ellen Tolmie © ACDI/CIDA; p. 21 bottom, p. 96 (3), p. 97 (5), p. 99 top left, p. 101 (3), p. 107 bottom Victor Englebert; p. 22 Embratur, Brazil; p. 23 top Patricio Baeza; p. 23 bottom, p. 99 bottom left, p. 99 bottom right, p. 107 middle Robin White/Fotolex; p. 24 bottom right U.S. Information Service; p. 25 top, 25 bottom right Richard Hartmier/Fotolex; p. 25 middle E.B. Waldock; p. 25 bottom left, p. 90 Courtesy of Costa Rica National Tourist Bureau; p. 27 Produced from USAF DMSP (Defense Meteorological Satellite Program) film transparencies archived for NOAA/NESDIS at the University of Colorado, CIRES/Campus Box 449, Boulder, CO 80309; p. 29 top, p. 31 middle left, p. 123 Industry, Science and Technology Canada; p. 29 middle Lee Battalia/United States Information Service; p. 29 bottom Courtesy of Alfonso Nieto, Press Attache, Consulado General de Mexico; p. 31 top left Dynese Griffiths/Network Stock Photo File; p. 31 top right Ministry of Natural Resources; p. 31 middle right Florida Department of Commerce, Division of Tourism; p. 31 bottom Bill Ivy; p. 37 Courtesy of the Department of Development, Government of Newfoundland and Labrador/Wayne Sturge; p. 37 Nova Scotia Tourism & Culture; p. 37 Prince Edward Island Tourism Photo/Wayne Barrett; p. 37 Keith Minchin/Visitors and Convention Bureau/Frederiction; p. 37 Metropolitan Toronto Convention & Visitors Association; p. 37 Alan Zenuk/Industry, Science and Technology Canada (Winnipeg); p. 37 Photo courtesy of the City of Edmonton; p. 37, p. 107 top M. Herweier (Victoria); p. 37 Bruce Sekulich/Government N.W.T.; p. 37, 85 left W. Towriss (Whitehorse); p. 39 bottom Ministry of Forests, Province of British Columbia; p. 42 top left Maynard Switzer; p. 42 bottom right Canapress Photo Service/Ryan Remiorz; p. 42 middle right Bob Anderson; p. 42 top right Mir Lada; p. 43 middle left The Toronto Star/P. Gower; p. 43 top left Canada Wide Feature Services/The Toronto Sun/Bill Sandford; p. 55 Department of Fisheries and Oceans, Pacific Region; p. 85 right Katsunori Nagase/Government N.W.T.; p. 85 bottom Tessa Macintosh/Government N.W.T.; p. 87 top left Photo courtesy of the Port Authority of New York and New Jersey; p. 87 top right Greater Houston Chamber of Commerce; p. 87 bottom San Francisco Convention and Visitors Bureau; p. 89 Mexican National Tourist Council; p. 91 © A. & J. Verkaik/Skyart; p. 92 G.L. Palacky; p. 99 top right, 101 bottom South African Tourism Board; p. 102 Canapress Photo; p. 106 left ACDI/CIDA; p. 106 right David Barbour © ACDI/CIDA; p. 108, 109 (2) Courtesy of the Australian Tourist Commission; p. 111 (2) Ian W.D. Dalziel; p. 113 top left, p. 122 (3), p. 123 top Indian and Northern Affairs Canada; p. 113 top right George Calef/Government N.W.T.; p. 113 bottom Lothar Dahlke/Government N.W.T.; p. 121 left "West Coast Indians Returning from the Hunt" by Thomas Mower Martin/Collection of Glenbow Museum, Calgary, Alberta 56.27.8; p. 121 right National Archives of Canada C-33615/"A Buffalo Pound" drawn by Lieut. Back, Engraved by Edw. Finden.

Contents

*Change is a major global expectation today. Atlas publishers are hard pressed to include the most recent boundary and name changes. All changes known at the time of printing have been included.

Introduction to Maps

Have you ever wondered where maps came from?

Long ago, soldiers, seamen, merchants, and other travellers created maps as a way of recording the places they had visited and the routes there and back. It is amazing how accurate some of those early maps were considering the tools used at the time by these mapmakers. Maps took shape slowly as people used them to find their way around. They became more and more accurate as mapmaking tools improved.

Believe it or not, some of the earliest maps were recorded on bark or animal skins. Others were burned or cut into bone or wood. Later maps were recorded on parchment, papyrus, or paper.

When collections of maps were joined together in one book, such as *The Macmillan School Atlas*, the book became known as an atlas. The idea of binding together a variety of up-to-date maps into a book began in Rome in the sixteenth century—over 400 years ago. It was the idea of a man named Antonio LaFriei, who saw an opportunity to create special map collections for his customers.

Atlases were named after the god Atlas of Greek mythology. Read a few Greek myths to find out why Atlas was doomed forever to carry the world on his shoulders.

Using an atlas is one way to find interesting and important information about places and people.

The Earth

When astronauts first landed on the moon, they looked back to Earth and saw a round, ball-like shape. From the moon, Earth looked like a giant globe of many colours. This proved again that the planet where you live is not flat, as was once thought, but is a **sphere**. Maps, however, are flat. Flat maps tell us many things about places on Earth. But only a globe correctly shows the size, shape, and position of land and water areas as they really are.

Many special locations are marked on a globe. Examine a globe carefully to discover the North and South Poles. Have you found them? Halfway between the poles is an imaginary line called the equator. The distance around the Earth at the equator is approximately 40 100 km. This distance is as far as travelling across Canada—seven times!

The Earth's **diameter** at the equator is roughly 12 760 km, while the diameter north to south is 12 710 km. As you can see by these measurements, the Earth is not perfectly round but is slightly flattened at the poles. However, because this flattening is so small compared with the Earth's total size, most people think of Earth as being ball-like in shape.

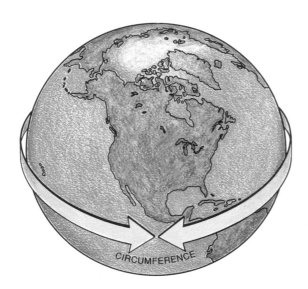

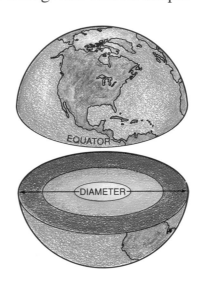

Hemispheres

How much of the globe can you see when you hold it in your hands? Only half of it shows at any one time. The half that you see is called a **hemisphere**, which means "half a sphere." No matter how you hold the globe, there will always be two hemispheres, the half that you see and the other half that you do not see.

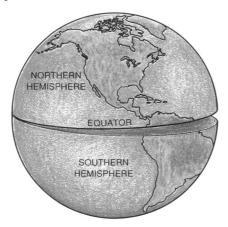

There can be many hemispheres. By moving the globe in your hands, you can see different halves. Remember there is always an opposite side to the one that you are looking at. When placed together, two hemispheres will always make a complete sphere.

If you could cut along the equator, the globe would separate into **northern** and **southern hemispheres**. If you could cut through the Atlantic and Pacific Oceans, then the globe would separate into the Eastern and Western Hemispheres.

Other important hemispheres are the **land hemisphere** and the **water hemisphere**. The land hemisphere is centred on a line drawn from Brussels to Paris. It contains almost 85 percent of all land on the Earth's surface. The centre of the water hemisphere is located near New Zealand.

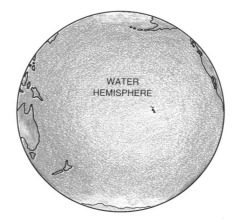

Latitude

Distances north and south of the equator are measured in degrees of latitude. Examine a globe and locate the equator again. The equator is the imaginary line that cuts the globe in half between the North and South Pole. Above and below the equator are other lines drawn in the same manner. Can you find them? These lines are parallel to the equator and are called **parallels of latitude**.

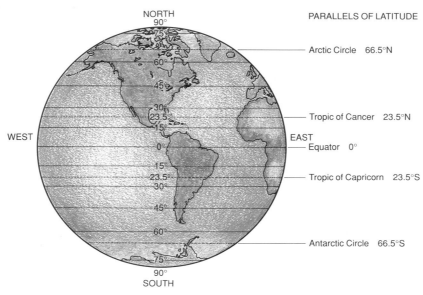

Each of the parallel lines of latitude are numbered in degrees. As you look at the lines above and below the equator, can you see that each parallel's number is followed by an N or S? This indicates whether you are looking at the Northern or Southern Hemisphere. The number of each parallel increases from 0° (the equator) to 90° as you move toward the North or South Pole. The latitude of the North Pole is 90°N. At the South Pole it is 90°S. No place on the globe can be more than 90° north or south. Why is this?

All locations along each parallel are the same distance from the equator. If the latitude of a place is 45°N, you know that place is on a line halfway between the equator and the North Pole. A place which has a latitude of 45°S is midway between the equator and the South Pole.

One degree of latitude is approximately 113 km. Once you know the latitude of any given position, you will be able to calculate its distance from the equator. Since all places along the same latitude are directly east or west of each other, parallels of latitude may be used to set east-west direction.

Some parallels have special names. Can you find the Arctic Circle and the Tropic of Cancer that lie north of the equator? The Antarctic Circle and the Tropic of Capricorn are south of it.

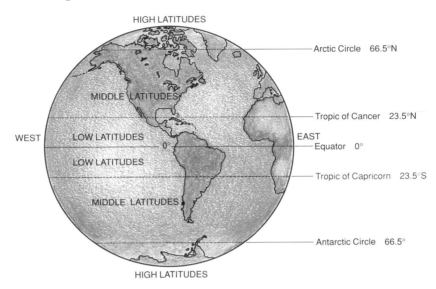

The parallels also divide the Earth into **low**, **middle**, and **high latitudes**.

Longitude

To help locate places on the Earth's surface, a second set of lines is drawn on a map or globe. These lines reach from the North to the South Pole.

They are called **meridians of longitude**. Unlike parallels of latitude, meridians are not parallel to one another but join at the poles. Can you see how each meridian is the same length as every other meridian?

Because there is no real difference between meridians, mapmakers had to agree upon which one to number 0. If you trace your finger along the line numbered 0, you will see that it passes through Greenwich, England. It is called the **prime meridian**. The meridian on the opposite side of the globe is called the **International Date Line**. Together, the prime meridian and the International Date Line divide the Earth into eastern and western hemispheres.

As you turn the globe in your hands you can see that the meridians of longitude are also numbered in degrees. Meridians measure distances in degrees east or west of the prime meridian. Going east of the prime meridian, the lines are numbered to 180°E. Going west they are numbered to 180°W.

The parallels of latitude and the meridians of longitude on maps together create a network of lines called a **grid**. A grid is used to locate particular places. When you know both the latitude and longitude of a given place, you are able to locate its exact position.

Even when a place is not located precisely where lines cross, you can still discover its approximate position. When using the grid for finding any given place, remember latitude is always stated before longitude. **Latitude and longitude give location.**

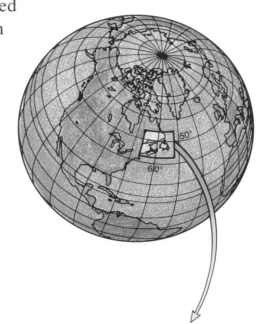

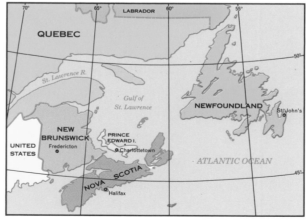

Gazetteer

At the back of the atlas is a section containing a list of all the names of places shown on the maps in this book. This section is called the **gazetteer** or **index**. A gazetteer includes all the information you need for locating places. Places are listed alphabetically. What other information are you given?

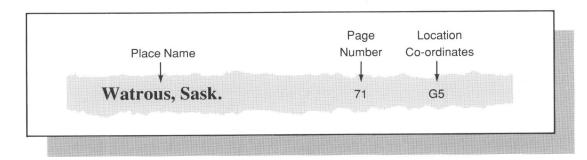

Place Name	Page Number	Location Co-ordinates
Watrous, Sask.	71	G5

Look in the gazetteer for the name of the place where you live. Use this information to locate your hometown on a map in the atlas. Try this activity again looking up places that you know about or that you have visited.

Great Circles

Every circle drawn around the globe divides it into two hemispheres. These circles are called Great Circles. The segment of a Great Circle that passes through any two places is the shortest distance between those places. Transportation pathways based on Great Circles are called **Great Circle Routes**.

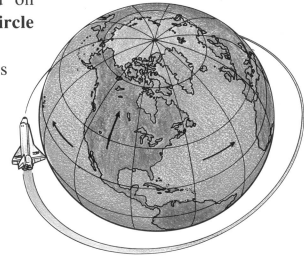

Ships often follow circle courses to reach their destination by the shortest possible route. Airplanes may follow circle routes over land unless they are forbidden to do so by certain countries.

Time

Every twenty-four hours the Earth makes one complete turn from west to east. It turns around an imaginary line that passes through the centre of the Earth from the North Pole to the South Pole. This line is known as the Earth's **axis**.

We depend on the Sun for our heat and our light. As the Earth spins on its axis, the part that faces the Sun receives heat and light. It is day on this part of the Earth. The part that is turned away from the Sun is cool and is in darkness. It is night on this part of the Earth.

Does the Sun really "rise in the east and set in the west"? No. The Sun never moves. Because the Earth turns on its axis from west to east, it may look as if the Sun were rising in the east. Our last view of the Sun is in the west, as the Earth turns away from it.

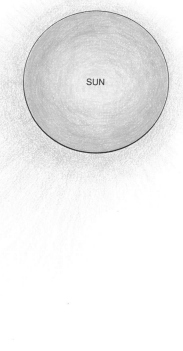

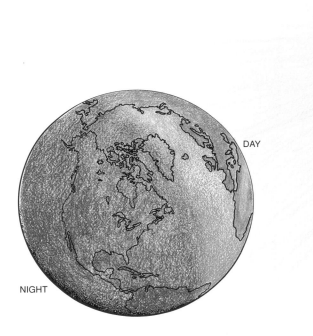

All places on Earth do not have noon at the same time, because of the way the Earth spins on its axis. Every twenty-four hours it turns 360° —15° each hour. Noon where you live would be one hour later than in a place fifteen degrees east of you.

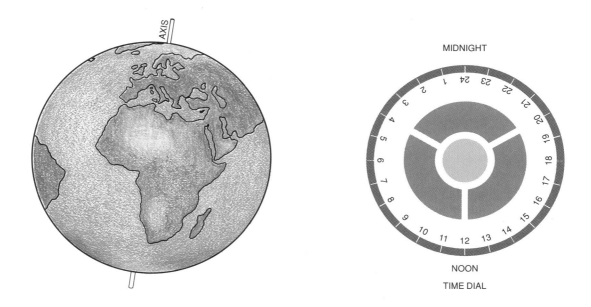

To avoid the confusion there would be if every place used its own time, **time zones** have been established. All places within a time zone have the same time. There are twenty-four of these time zones — one for every fifteen degrees.

The borders of time zones do not always follow meridians, but often follow the borders of countries or of provinces and states.

Canada's time zones are shown on the map below.

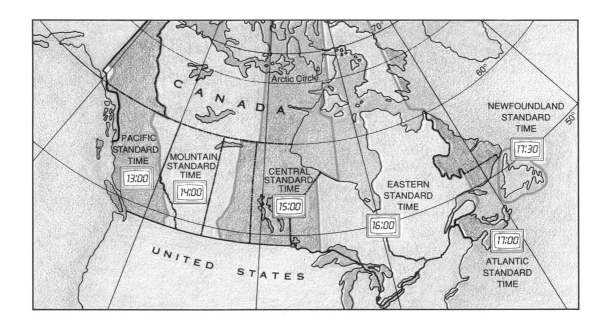

The Change of Seasons

As the Earth revolves in an orbit about the Sun, its axis is tilted at an angle of 23.5°. This causes changes in the length of time places receive heat and sunlight. That is why seasons change each year. In summer, the Northern Hemisphere tilts toward the Sun to receive its direct rays. As a result the days are longer and have greater heat. In winter, the Northern Hemisphere tilts away from the Sun. Then the days are shorter and have less heat. In spring and fall the Earth's axis points neither toward nor away from the Sun.

In the Southern Hemisphere the seasons are opposite to our own. Look at a globe and see if you can explain why this happens.

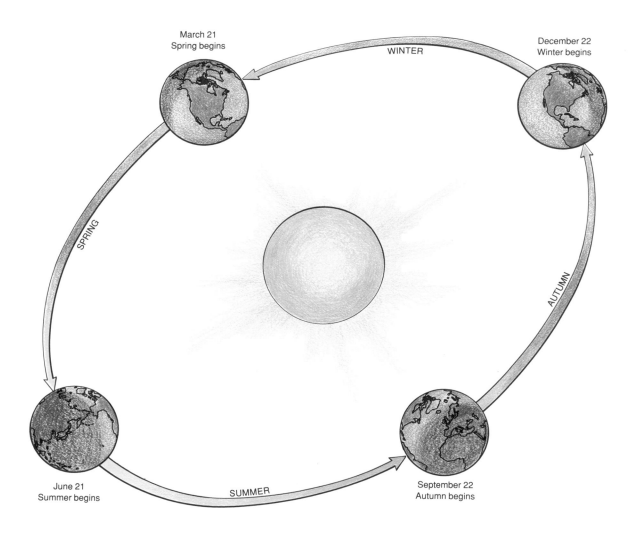

March 21
Spring begins

December 22
Winter begins

WINTER

SPRING

AUTUMN

June 21
Summer begins

SUMMER

September 22
Autumn begins

The Earth and the Moon

The Moon is the brightest object in our night sky. When you look at it from Earth it seems to be as large as the Sun. But it is not as large as the Sun. It looks larger only because it is closer to Earth. The Moon's distance from Earth is about 384 400 km. This is about ten times the distance around the Earth at its equator.

If you were watching the Moon through a telescope, you would see that it travels from west to east. As it travels, the Moon appears to change its shape. These changes are called **phases** of the Moon.

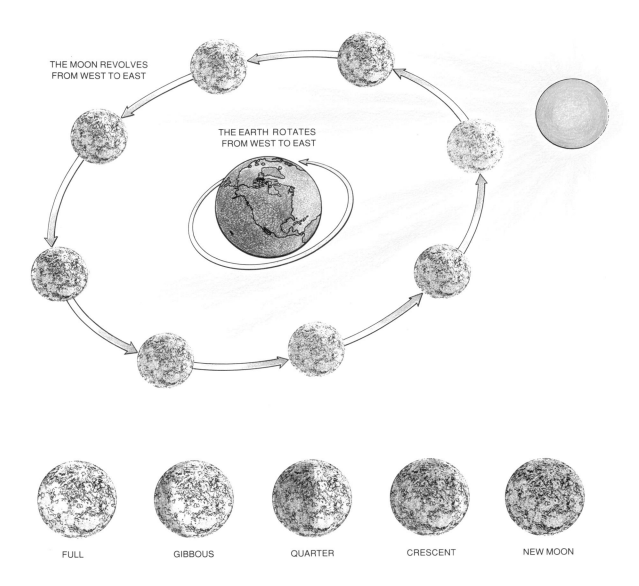

THE MOON REVOLVES FROM WEST TO EAST

THE EARTH ROTATES FROM WEST TO EAST

FULL   GIBBOUS   QUARTER   CRESCENT   NEW MOON

Mapping

A **map** is a drawing of all or a part of the Earth's surface seen as if you were looking down on it from above. Maps attempt to present Earth's natural or built features on a flat surface. We know a globe gives us the truest picture of any land or water area, but we also know it is not as convenient to use as a map is. Imagine taking a globe along with you every time you and your family went on a special trip!

Mapmakers have tried many different ways of drawing the rounded surface of Earth on a flat piece of paper. But they have discovered that no matter what way they tried, they could not flatten a curved surface without causing changes to the shape of the continents.

The globe is the only way of showing how the Earth looks to true scale. The diagram below shows one way to make a map. If a globe were cut open along its lines of latitude and longitude and then pressed flat, it would be a map.

 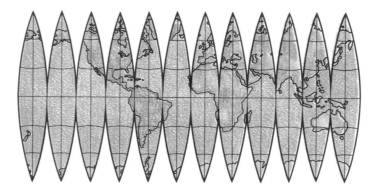

Map Projections

Each different way of transferring details from a globe to a sheet of paper is called a **map projection.** There are many kinds of map projections; each one is designed for a special reason. The illustrations on page 13 show three different styles of map projections: the Robinson projection, the Mercator projection, and the Peters projection.

Mapmakers often use mathematics to work out a projection. Can you see how in each illustration the shapes of the continents differ from the way they appear on the globe? These changes are called **distortions.** There is no way to make a flat map without some distortion.

Robinson projection

National Geographic uses this projection that has a distortion of less than 20 percent for most of the world continents.

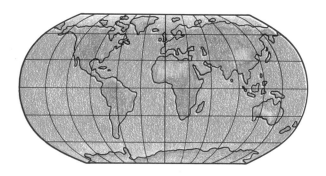

Mercator projection

Navigators and pilots prefer to use this projection because the great circle routes are shown as straight lines rather than as curved lines. However, note how northern and southern latitudes appear very much bigger than they really are.

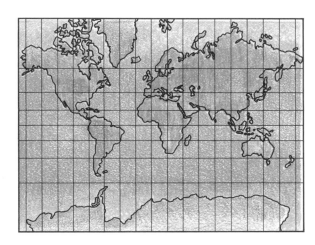

Peters projection

The United Nations prefers this projection because it shows developing countries clearly. All countries are shown with accurate areas but, as you can see, some shapes are distorted.

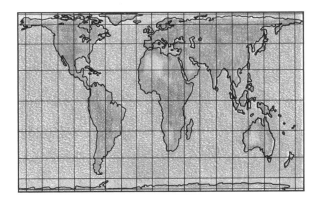

When you examine maps in this atlas, you will see differences from one map to another. For example, even using the same projection, maps of a large area (such as that found on page 28) will show more distortion than maps of a smaller area (page 71). Why do you suppose that happens?

No single projection can be drawn to show accurately all four qualities—area, shape, distance, and direction—at the same time. Only a globe can do that.

Understanding Maps

There are different kinds of maps. Some maps are designed to show you where certain places are in the world. These are called **general maps**. Other maps show specific information about things such as transportation routes or what vegetation is like in a certain area. These are called **thematic maps**. Information on a thematic map is usually coded with colour and shapes.

An example of a general map can be found on page 36. An example of a thematic map can be found on page 38. Can you find other examples?

Scale

It would be impossible to draw a map the same size as the area it shows. Imagine how much paper you would need to map your city or town! For this reason, all maps are drawn to **scale**. An exact distance on the map stands for a certain (much larger) distance on the ground. Every map has some statement of scale to help you estimate distances.

Maps are drawn to different scales. One map may show an area twice as large as the area shown on another map. A one-page map of a large area of land and water, such as Canada, must be drawn to a small scale, so that the large area will fit on the page. A one-page map of a much smaller area, such as Manitoba, can be drawn at a larger scale. A large-scale map shows more detail. Look at Manitoba on atlas page 36 and on page 69. What difference do you see? What is the scale of each of these maps?

Scale is shown in various ways. A linear scale uses a rule or line divided into equal segments. Each segment represents a specific distance on the ground. A second method states the scale as the ratio between the actual distance and the distance on the map. If a mapped area was drawn at one

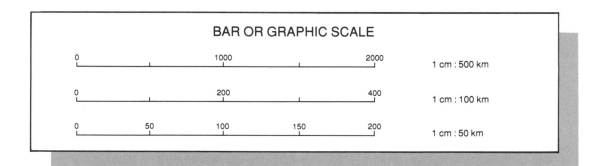

BAR OR GRAPHIC SCALE

| 0 | 1000 | 2000 | 1 cm : 500 km |

| 0 | 200 | 400 | 1 cm : 100 km |

| 0 | 50 | 100 | 150 | 200 | 1 cm : 50 km |

quarter the actual size, the ratio would be expressed at 1:4. If an area was mapped at one thousandth of its actual size, the ratio would be 1:1000. A third method of expressing scale is simply in a statement: "One centimetre represents ten kilometres.

Unless you look closely, the linear scales on maps may all look the same. The line used for the scales on the maps may all be the same length. But this length may represent entirely different distances from map to map. On one map 1 cm might represent 100 km. On a second map a line of exactly the same length might represent only 50 km. See how many different linear scales you can find in this atlas.

Legend

Different maps give different kinds of information. To find out what a map is all about, look at its title. The title will tell you the name of the area or region shown on the map, and what kind of map it is that you are looking at. The **legend** will explain the symbols used on the map.

Each **colour** used on a map usually has its own special meaning. But every map has its own special colouring. A colour used on one map may mean something completely different when used on another map.

A legend shows the **symbols** used on the map. They may represent natural features such as a river or a lake, or features made by humans such as a road or a pulp and paper mill.

Map symbols change meaning from one map to another, just the way colours do. It is very important to use the legend if you want to uncover the information on each map.

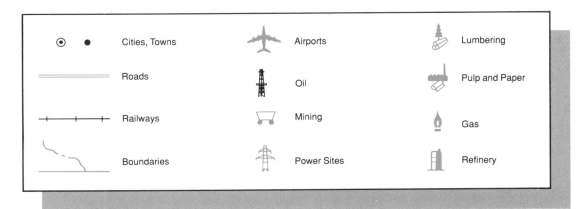

Example of a Legend

Elevation

When mapmakers want to show different heights of land on their maps, they use **contour lines**. Contour lines join together places of the same height. The spaces between the contour lines show heights which are at the same level. Where the contour lines are very close together the slope of the land is steeper than in areas where the contour lines are widely spaced.

Look at these pictures carefully. Can you see that the heights of land are not the same everywhere? Some lands are slightly above sea level. These are called **lowlands**. Other lands are higher and are called **middlelands**. The highest lands are called **highlands**.

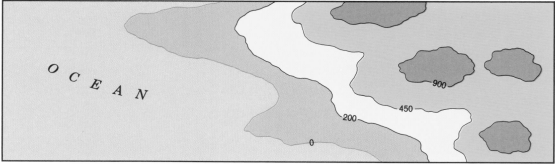

Above you see a map of the same area. Can you find all the places where the land 200 m above sea level is joined by the same line? Follow this line with your finger to make a complete circle.

Colour

Colour is often used to show heights of land. All the land from sea level at 0 m to 200 m above sea level is shown in this atlas as green. The land 200 m to 450 m is coloured yellow. The land 450 m to 900 m is brown. What colour is used when showing heights of land above 900 m?

Direction

Because a large map is usually hung on a wall, you may make the mistake of thinking direction north is always at the top of the map. But "up" and north on a map may not necessarily be the same thing.

This is why most maps have a special symbol to show **direction**. In this atlas the direction north is shown like this.

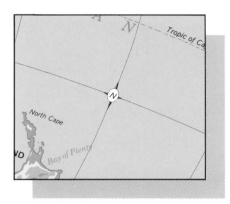

Once you know where north is, you should know where all the other directions are for that particular map. Can you find them? When you face north, south is in the opposite direction, east is to the right. Where is west?

You can use the grid lines of a map to find the four main directions too. Parallels of latitude always lie in an east-west direction. All meridians of longitude run in a north-south direction.

Summary

Maps tell you about people and places in the world. The globe is a map of the Earth, and is the same shape as the Earth itself. Flat maps of the Earth, or part of it, are often collected together in an atlas.

The size, shape, or area of features on the Earth may be distorted when they are projected onto a flat map. On both globes and flat maps, lines of latitude and longitude help you to find the location of places.

All maps have a title and a legend to help you read the map. These tell you what the map is about, and what the symbols and colours used on the map represent. All maps also have a scale.

Geographic Terms

This is a view of an area that includes the main features found on the Earth's surface.

PEAK

MOUNTAINS

PASS

DIVIDE

SLOPE

VALLEY

River

HILL

LOWLANDS

Coastline

PENINSULA

Stream

Lake

FOOTHILLS

Delta

Inlet

Bay

Gulf

Tributary

Town

Railway

Stream

Cape

Archipelago

River

Bridge

Strait

Road

Road

CITY

Lagoon

Bridge

BASIN

Road

Harbour

Reef

Canal

Highway

Swamp

Town

Creek

PLAIN

River Mouth

Village

Airport

Beach

Isthmus

Bay

Bluff

Cape

Gulf

Lighthouse

Rocks

Headland

Strait

Rocks

SEA

ISLAND

Mountains

Foothills

Lowlands

A map of the view shown on the opposite page would look like this.

PASS

MOUNTAIN
• PEAK

DIVIDE

SLOPE

PENINSULA

River

HILL

LOWLANDS

Coastline

VALLEY
Stream

Lake

FOOTHILLS

Railway

Delta

Inlet

Sea

Tributary

River

Town

Cape

Strait

Archipelago

Lagoon

BASIN

Road

Harbour

CITY

Bay

Reef

Bridge

Bridge

Town

Highway

Airport

Creek

Canal

PLAIN

Road

Swamp

River Mouth

Village

Bay

Beach

Isthmus

Gulf

Lighthouse

Rocks

Strait

Island

Bluff

Headland

Rocks

LEGEND

	Highway
	Road
	Railway
	City
●	Town
•	Village
✳	Lighthouse
)(	Bridge
◢	Airport

Plains.

Valleys

Rivers

The World
POLITICAL DIVISIONS

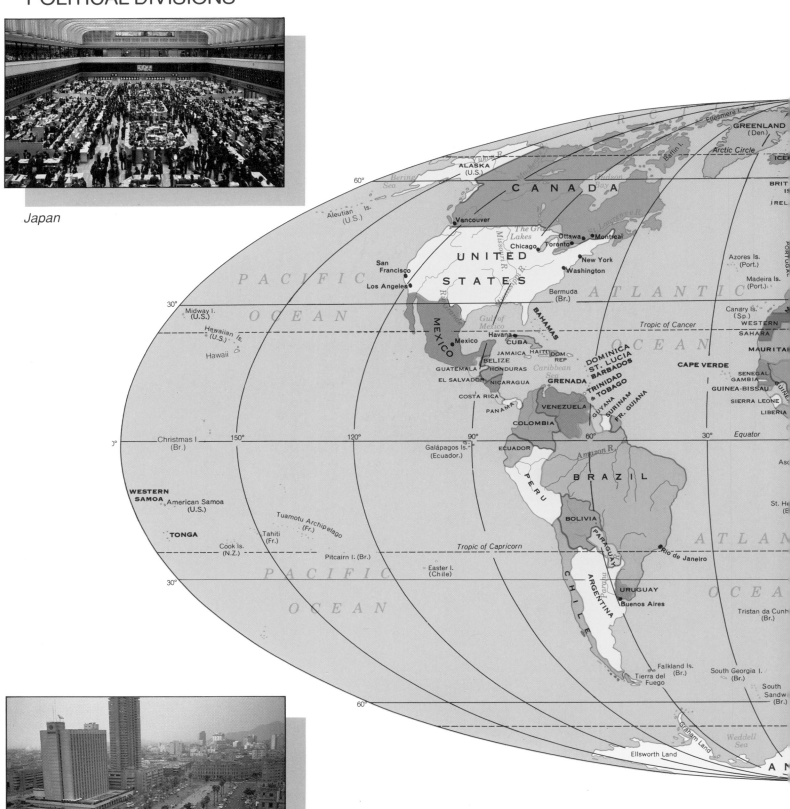

Japan

Peru

ARCTIC

Ellesmere I.

GREENLAND
(Den.)

Arctic Circle

ICE

Yukon R.

ALASKA
(U.S.)

Baffin I.

Hudson
Bay

BRIT

C A N A D A

Mackenzie R.

Lawrence R.

IREL

*Bering
Sea*

60°

Vancouver

*The Great
Lakes*

Ottawa Montreal

Toronto

Chicago

New York

Azores Is.
(Port.)

PORTUGA

P A C I F I C

San
Francisco

U N I T E D

Washington

Madeira Is.
(Port.)

Los Angeles

S T A T E S

Bermuda
(Br.)

A T L A N T I C

30°

Midway I.
(U.S.)

O C E A N

Rio Grande

Gulf of
Mexico

Tropic of Cancer

Canary Is.
(Sp.)

WESTERN

Hawaiian Is.
(U.S.)

MEXICO

Mexico

Havana

CUBA

O C E A N

SAHARA

Hawaii

JAMAICA HAITI DOM
REP

DOMINICA
ST. LUCIA

MAURITA

BELIZE

BARBADOS

CAPE VERDE

GUATEMALA HONDURAS

*Caribbean
Sea*

SENEGAL
GAMBIA

EL SALVADOR NICARAGUA

GRENADA

TRINIDAD
& TOBAGO

GUINEA-BISSAU

COSTA RICA

GUYANA

SIERRA LEONE

PANAMA

VENEZUELA

SURINAM
FR. GUIANA

LIBERIA

COLOMBIA

60°

30°

Equator

0°

Christmas I.
(Br.)

150°

120°

90°

Galápagos Is.
(Ecuador.)

ECUADOR

Amazon R.

B R A Z I L

Asc

WESTERN
SAMOA

American Samoa
(U.S.)

PERU

St. He
(B

BOLIVIA

Tuamotu Archipelago
(Fr.)

TONGA

Tahiti
(Fr.)

PARAGUAY

A T L A N

Cook Is.
(N.Z.)

Tropic of Capricorn

Rio de Janeiro

Pitcairn I. (Br.)

Easter I.
(Chile)

CHILE

ARGENTINA

URUGUAY

O C E A

30°

P A C I F I C

Paraná R.

Buenos Aires

Tristan da Cunh
(Br.)

O C E A N

Falkland Is.
(Br.)

South Georgia I.
(Br.)

Tierra del
Fuego

South
Sandw
(Br.)

60°

Graham Land

Weddell
Sea

Ellsworth Land

AN

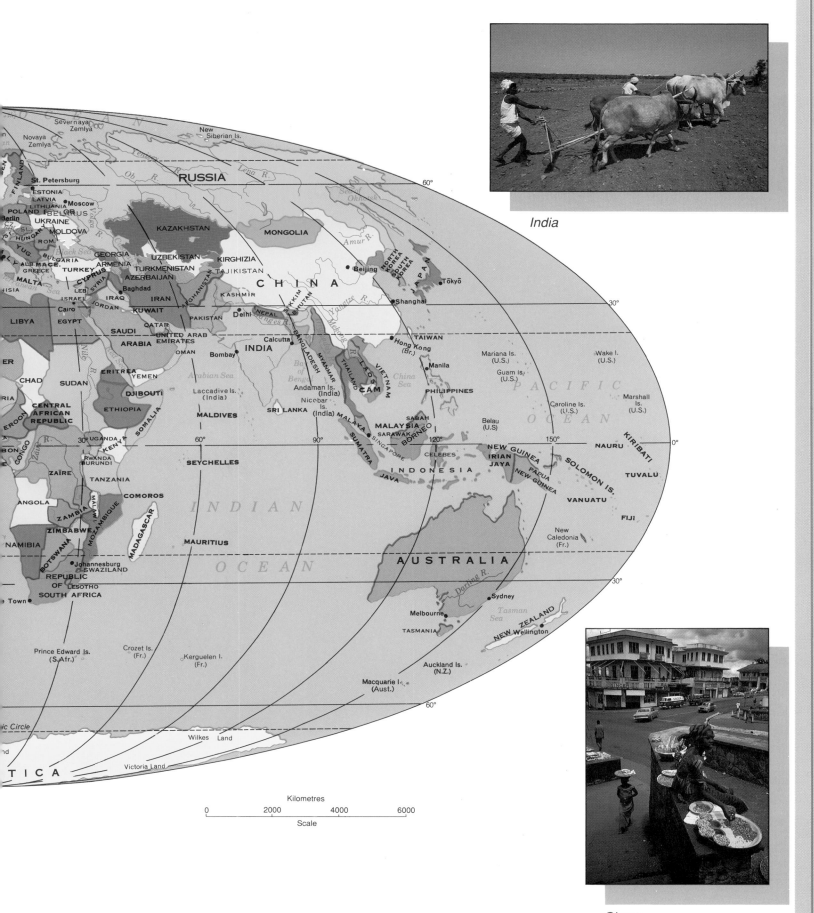

India

Ghana

Map labels

Severnaya Zemlya
New Siberian Is.
Novaya Zemlya
FINLAND
St. Petersburg
RUSSIA
60°
ESTONIA
LATVIA
Moscow
LITHUANIA
POLAND
BELARUS
UKRAINE
MOLDOVA
HUNG.
YUG.
ROM.
BULGARIA
ALB.
MACE.
GREECE
MALTA
TURKEY
CYPRUS
ISRAEL
LEB.
SYRIA
JORDAN
IRAQ
Baghdad
Cairo
EGYPT
LIBYA
KUWAIT
QATAR
SAUDI ARABIA
UNITED ARAB EMIRATES
OMAN
YEMEN
CHAD
SUDAN
ERITREA
DJIBOUTI
ETHIOPIA
CENTRAL AFRICAN REPUBLIC
SOMALIA
UGANDA
30°
KENYA
CONGO
ZAÏRE
RWANDA
BURUNDI
TANZANIA
ANGOLA
ZAMBIA
MALAWI
MOZAMBIQUE
COMOROS
ZIMBABWE
MADAGASCAR
NAMIBIA
BOTSWANA
SWAZILAND
Johannesburg
REPUBLIC OF SOUTH AFRICA
LESOTHO
Town

KAZAKHSTAN
MONGOLIA
GEORGIA
ARMENIA
UZBEKISTAN
KIRGHIZIA
TURKMENISTAN
TAJIKISTAN
AZERBAIJAN
AFGHANISTAN
IRAN
PAKISTAN
KASHMIR
Delhi
NEPAL
SIKKIM
BHUTAN
BANGLADESH
Calcutta
INDIA
Bombay
Laccadive Is. (India)
MALDIVES
SRI LANKA
Andaman Is. (India)
Nicobar Is. (India)
MYANMAR
THAILAND
LAOS
VIETNAM
CAM
MALAYA
MALAYSIA
SABAH
SARAWAK
SINGAPORE
BORNEO
SUMATRA
JAVA
INDONESIA
CELEBES

CHINA
Beijing
NORTH KOREA
SOUTH KOREA
JAPAN
Tōkyō
Shanghai
30°
TAIWAN
Hong Kong (Br.)
Manila
China Sea
PHILIPPINES
Mariana Is. (U.S.)
Guam Is. (U.S.)
Wake I. (U.S.)
Caroline Is. (U.S.)
Marshall Is. (U.S.)
Belau (U.S)
NEW GUINEA
IRIAN JAYA
PAPUA NEW GUINEA
SOLOMON IS.
NAURU
KIRIBATI
0°
TUVALU
VANUATU
FIJI
New Caledonia (Fr.)
PACIFIC OCEAN

INDIAN OCEAN
SEYCHELLES
MAURITIUS

AUSTRALIA
Darling R.
Sydney
Melbourne
TASMANIA
Tasman Sea
NEW ZEALAND
Wellington
30°

Prince Edward Is. (S.Afr.)
Crozet Is. (Fr.)
Kerguelen I. (Fr.)
Auckland Is. (N.Z.)
Macquarie I. (Aust.)
60°

ic Circle
Wilkes Land
Victoria Land
TICA

Ob R.
Lena R.
Amur R.
Sea of Okhotsk
Yangtze R.
Ganges R.
Mekong R.
Bay of Bengal
Arabian Sea
Nile R.
Congo R.
Black Sea
Volga

Kilometres
0   2000   4000   6000
Scale

The World
LANDFORMS–Relief

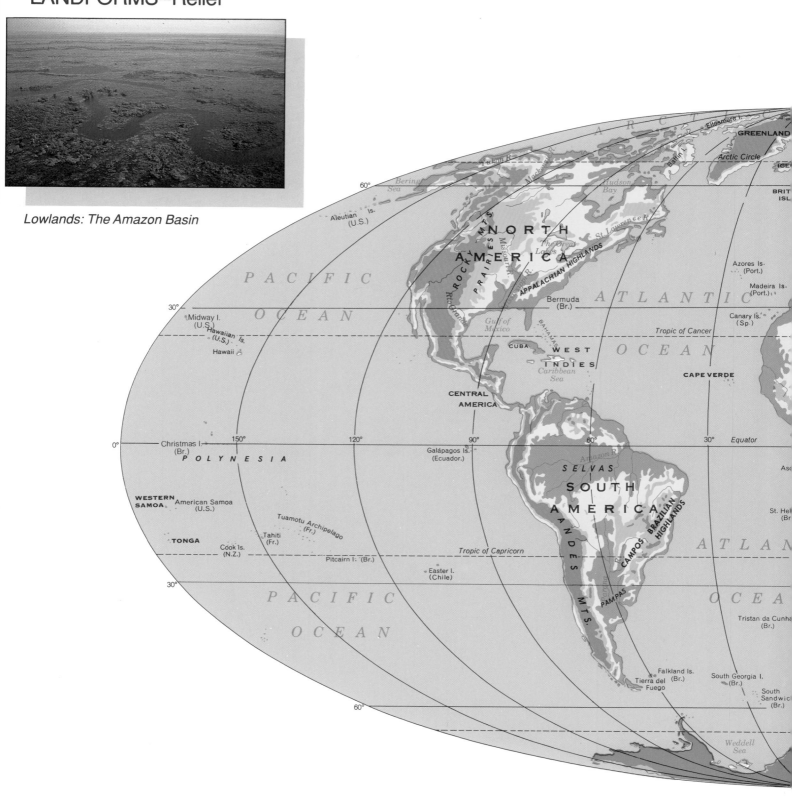

Lowlands: The Amazon Basin

Map labels:
ARCTI

Ellesmere I.
GREENLAND
Baffin I.
Arctic Circle
ICE
60°
Bering Sea
Mackenzie R.
Hudson Bay
BRIT ISL
Aleutian Is. (U.S.)
ROCKY MTS
NORTH AMERICA
Missouri R.
PRAIRIES
The Great Lakes
St. Lawrence R.
APPALACHIAN HIGHLANDS
Azores Is. (Port.)
30°
Rio Grande
Bermuda (Br.)
Madeira Is. (Port.)
PACIFIC OCEAN
ATLANTIC OCEAN
Midway I. (U.S.)
Gulf of Mexico
Tropic of Cancer
Canary Is. (Sp.)
Hawaiian Is. (U.S.)
CUBA
WEST INDIES
BAHAMAS
Hawaii
Caribbean Sea
CAPE VERDE
CENTRAL AMERICA
0°
Christmas I. (Br.)
150°
120°
90°
Galápagos Is. (Ecuador.)
60°
30°
Equator
Asc
POLYNESIA
Amazon R.
SELVAS
St. Hel (Br
WESTERN SAMOA
American Samoa (U.S.)
SOUTH AMERICA
Tuamotu Archipelago (Fr.)
BRAZILIAN HIGHLANDS
ATLAN
TONGA
Tahiti (Fr.)
CAMPOS
Cook Is. (N.Z.)
Tropic of Capricorn
ANDES MTS
OCEA
Pitcairn I. (Br.)
PAMPAS
Easter I. (Chile)
30°
Tristan da Cunha (Br.)
PACIFIC OCEAN
Falkland Is. (Br.)
South Georgia I. (Br.)
Tierra del Fuego
South Sandwich (Br.)
60°
Weddell Sea

Legend:
Lowlands (0 m to 200 m)
Middlelands (200 m to 450 m)
Highlands (Over 450 m)

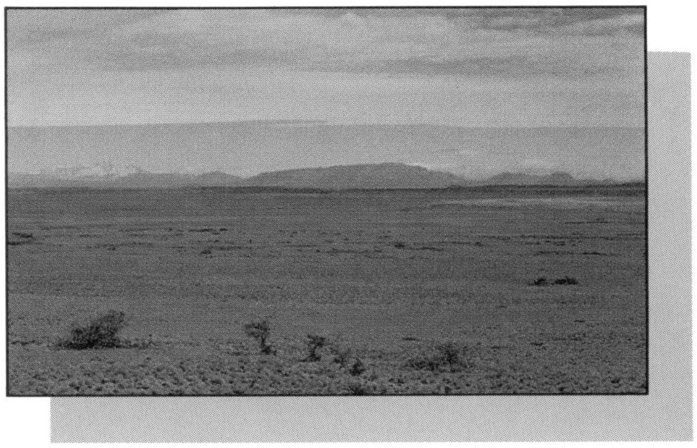

Middlelands: The Pampas, Argentina

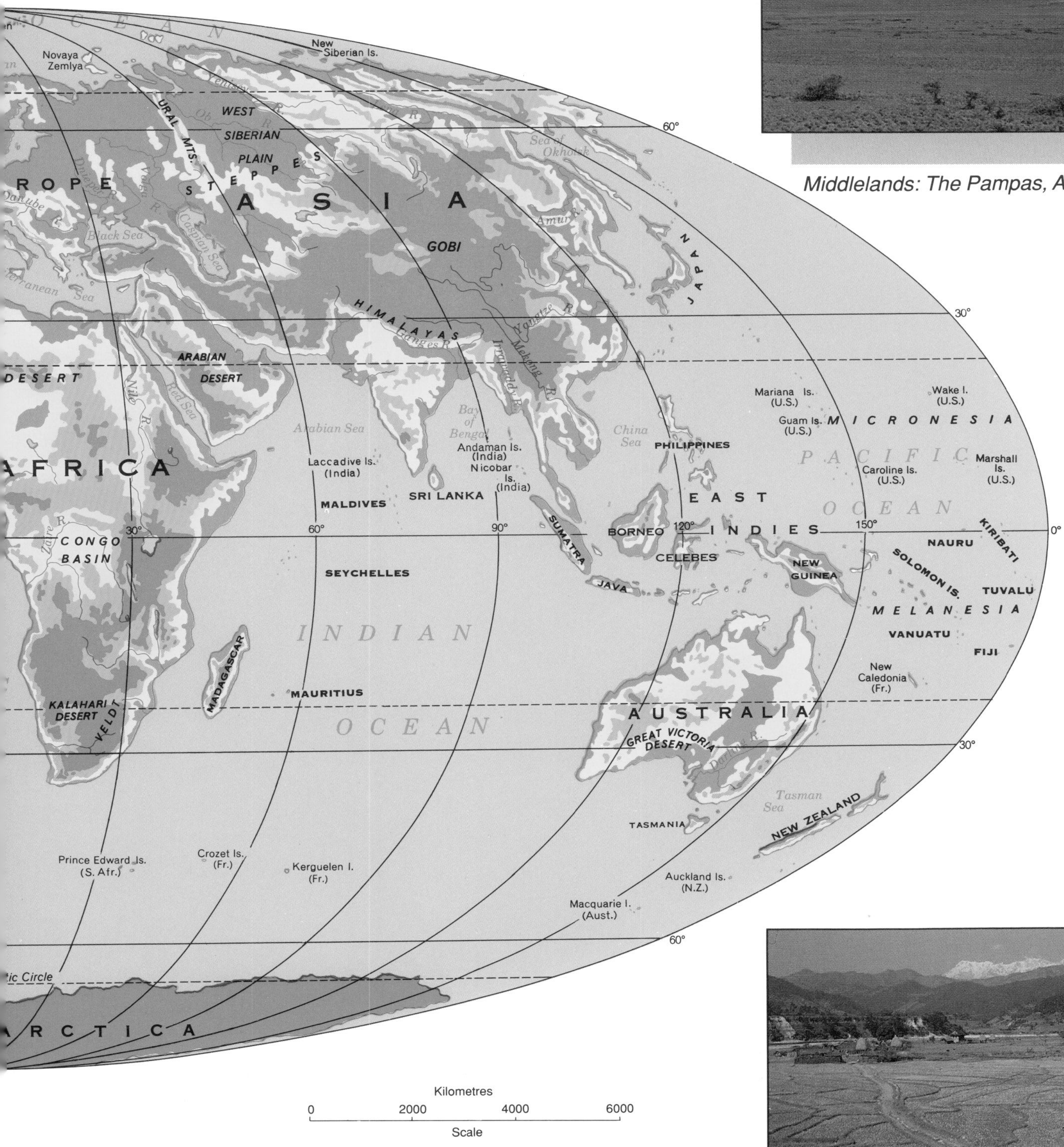

New Siberian Is.
Novaya Zemlya
URAL MTS.
WEST SIBERIAN PLAIN
STEPPES
Sea of Okhotsk
A S I A
Amur R.
Black Sea
Caspian Sea
GOBI
JAPAN
HIMALAYAS
Ganges R.
Yangtze R.
Mekong R.
Irrawaddy R.
ARABIAN DESERT
Red Sea
Nile R.
Arabian Sea
Bay of Bengal
China Sea
PHILIPPINES
Mariana Is. (U.S.)
Guam Is. (U.S.)
Wake I. (U.S.)
MICRONESIA
PACIFIC OCEAN
Marshall Is. (U.S.)
Caroline Is. (U.S.)
Laccadive Is. (India)
Andaman Is. (India)
Nicobar Is. (India)
MALDIVES
SRI LANKA
EAST INDIES
SUMATRA
BORNEO
CELEBES
JAVA
NEW GUINEA
NAURU
KIRIBATI
SOLOMON IS.
TUVALU
MELANESIA
VANUATU
FIJI
New Caledonia (Fr.)
CONGO BASIN
Zaire R.
SEYCHELLES
MADAGASCAR
INDIAN OCEAN
MAURITIUS
KALAHARI DESERT
VELDT
AUSTRALIA
GREAT VICTORIA DESERT
Darling R.
Tasman Sea
NEW ZEALAND
TASMANIA
Prince Edward Is. (S. Afr.)
Crozet Is. (Fr.)
Kerguelen I. (Fr.)
Auckland Is. (N.Z.)
Macquarie I. (Aust.)
Antarctic Circle
60°
30°
0°
90°
120°
150°
Kilometres
0
2000
4000
6000
Scale

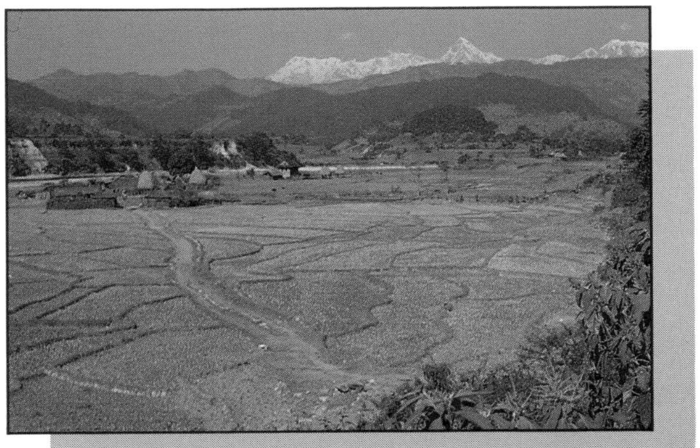

Highlands: The Himalayas, Nepal

The World
VEGETATION

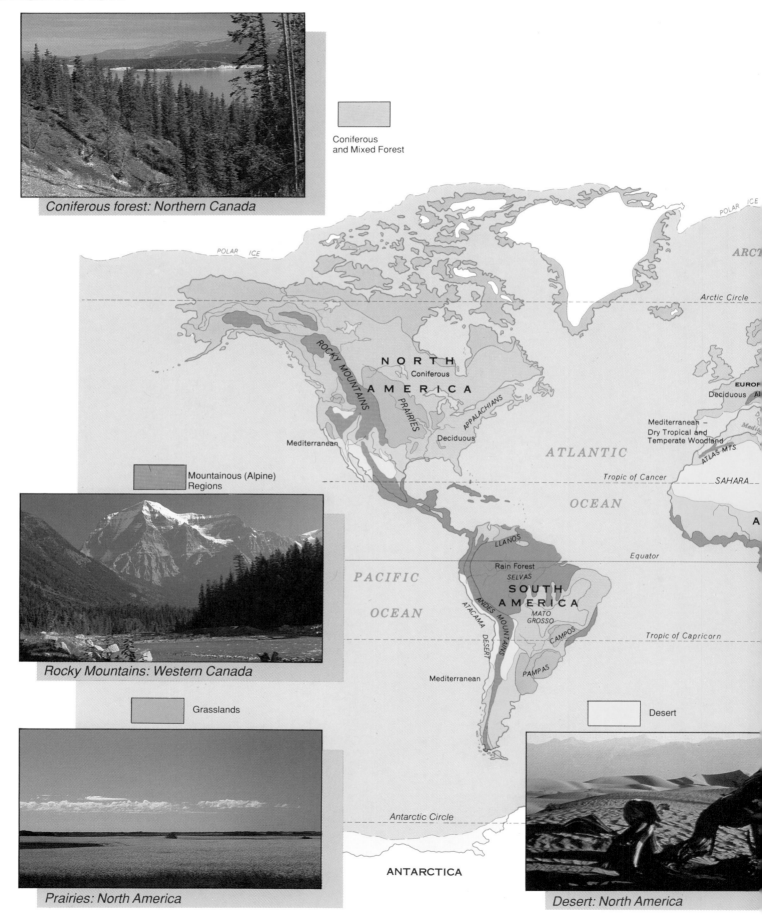

Coniferous forest: Northern Canada

Coniferous
and Mixed Forest

Mountainous (Alpine)
Regions

Rocky Mountains: Western Canada

Grasslands

Desert

Prairies: North America

Desert: North America

POLAR ICE

POLAR ICE

ARCT

Arctic Circle

NORTH
AMERICA
Coniferous

ROCKY MOUNTAINS

PRAIRIES

APPALACHIANS

Deciduous

Mediterranean

EUROP
Deciduous Al

Mediterranean –
Dry Tropical and
Temperate Woodland

ATLAS MTS.

SAHARA

A

ATLANTIC

OCEAN

Tropic of Cancer

Mediter

PACIFIC

OCEAN

LLANOS

Rain Forest

SELVAS

SOUTH
AMERICA

ANDES MOUNTAINS

ATACAMA DESERT

MATO
GROSSO

CAMPOS

PAMPAS

Mediterranean

Equator

Tropic of Capricorn

Antarctic Circle

ANTARCTICA

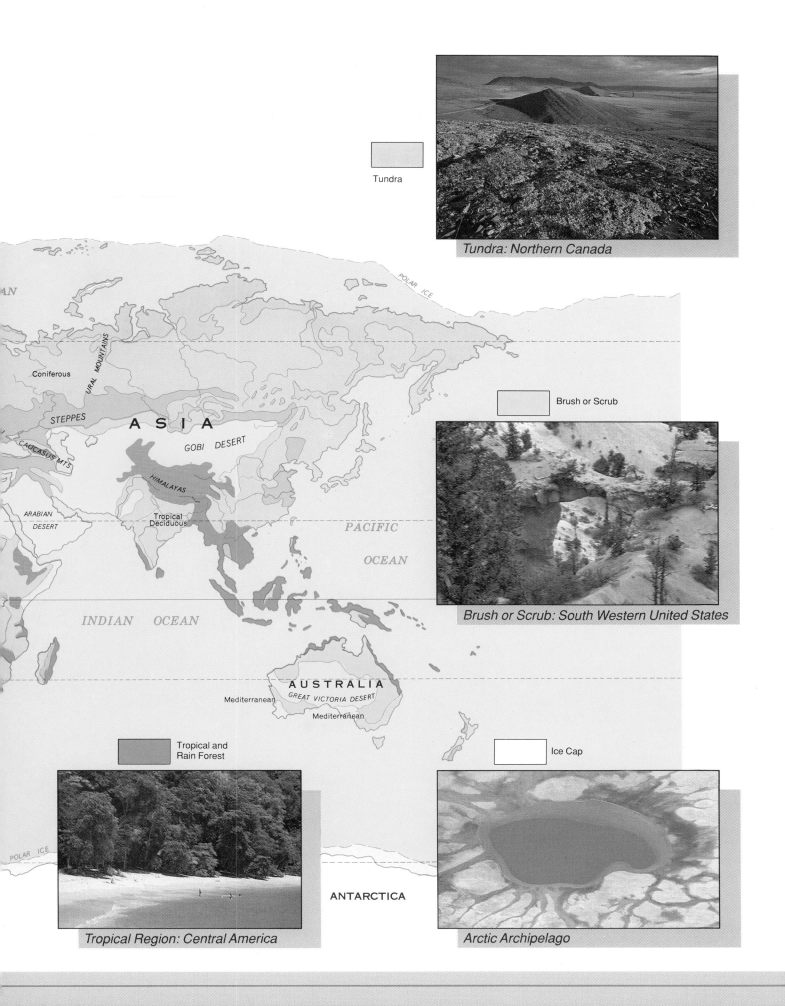

Tundra

Tundra: Northern Canada

Brush or Scrub

Brush or Scrub: South Western United States

Coniferous

URAL MOUNTAINS

STEPPES

A S I A

CAUCASUS MTS

GOBI DESERT

HIMALAYAS

ARABIAN
DESERT

Tropical
Deciduous

POLAR ICE

PACIFIC

OCEAN

INDIAN OCEAN

AUSTRALIA

GREAT VICTORIA DESERT

Mediterranean

Mediterranean

Tropical and
Rain Forest

Ice Cap

POLAR ICE

ANTARCTICA

Tropical Region: Central America

Arctic Archipelago

The World
HEMISPHERES

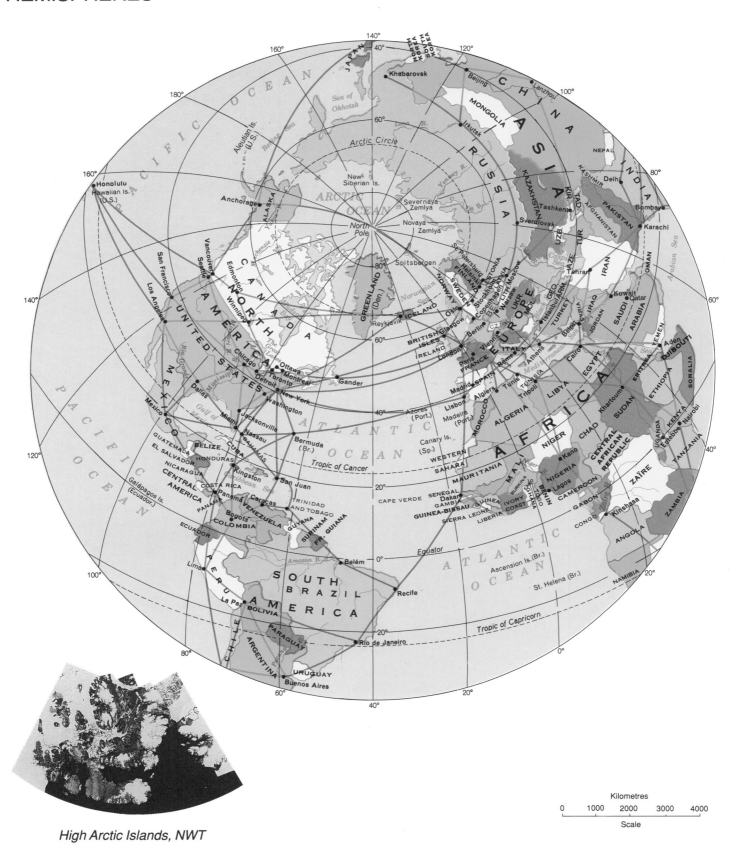

High Arctic Islands, NWT

Kilometres

0   1000   2000   3000   4000

Scale

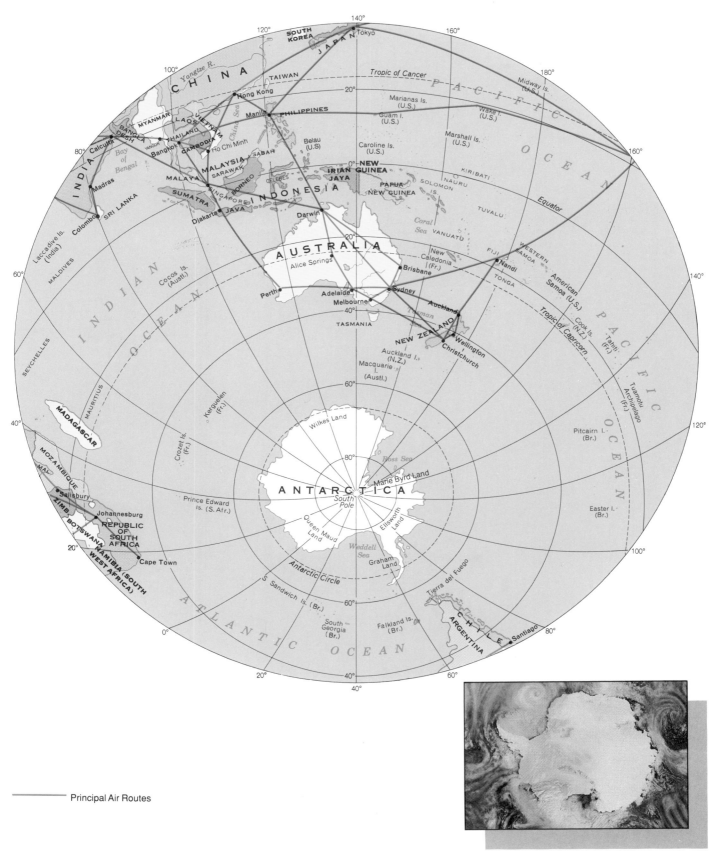

CHINA
SOUTH KOREA
JAPAN
Tokyo
Yangtze R.
TAIWAN
Tropic of Cancer
PACIFIC OCEAN
Midway Is. (U.S.)
Hong Kong
Marianas Is.
180°
MYANMAR
LAOS
VIETNAM
Manila
PHILIPPINES
Guam I. (U.S.)
Wake I. (U.S.)
BANGLA-DESH
YANGON
THAILAND
CAMBODIA
Ho Chi Minh
Belau (U.S)
Caroline Is. (U.S.)
Marshall Is. (U.S.)
Calcutta
Bangkok
MALAYSIA
SARAWAK
SABAH
NEW IRIAN JAYA
KIRIBATI
160°
INDIA
Madras
MALAYA
SINGAPORE
BORNEO
CELEBES
INDONESIA
PAPUA NEW GUINEA
NAURU
SOLOMON Is.
Equator
SRI LANKA
SUMATRA
JAVA
Djakarta
Darwin
Coral Sea
VANUATU
TUVALU
Laccadive Is. (India)
Colombo
MALDIVES
INDIAN OCEAN
Cocos Is. (Austl.)
AUSTRALIA
Alice Springs
New Caledonia (Fr.)
FIJI
Nandi
WESTERN SAMOA
American Samoa (U.S.)
140°
SEYCHELLES
Perth
Adelaide
Melbourne
Brisbane
Sydney
Auckland
TONGA
Cook Is. (N.Z.)
Tahiti (Fr.)
Tropic of Capricorn
TASMANIA
NEW ZEALAND
Wellington
Christchurch
Tuamotu Archipelago (Fr.)
MADAGASCAR
MAURITIUS
Kerguelen (Fr.)
Auckland I. (N.Z.)
Macquarie I. (Austl.)
Pitcairn I. (Br.)
120°
MOZAMBIQUE
MAL
Crozet Is. (Fr.)
Wilkes Land
Ross Sea
Easter I. (Br.)
Salisbury
ZIMB
BOTSWANA
REPUBLIC OF SOUTH AFRICA
Johannesburg
Prince Edward Is. (S. Afr.)
ANTARCTICA
Marie Byrd Land
South Pole
Ellsworth Land
NAMIBIA (SOUTH WEST AFRICA)
Cape Town
Queen Maud Land
Weddell Sea
Graham Land
100°
ATLANTIC OCEAN
S. Sandwich Is. (Br.)
Antarctic Circle
S. Georgia (Br.)
Falkland Is. (Br.)
Tierra del Fuego
CHILE
ARGENTINA
Santiago
PACIFIC OCEAN

Principal Air Routes

Antarctica

North America
POLITICAL DIVISIONS

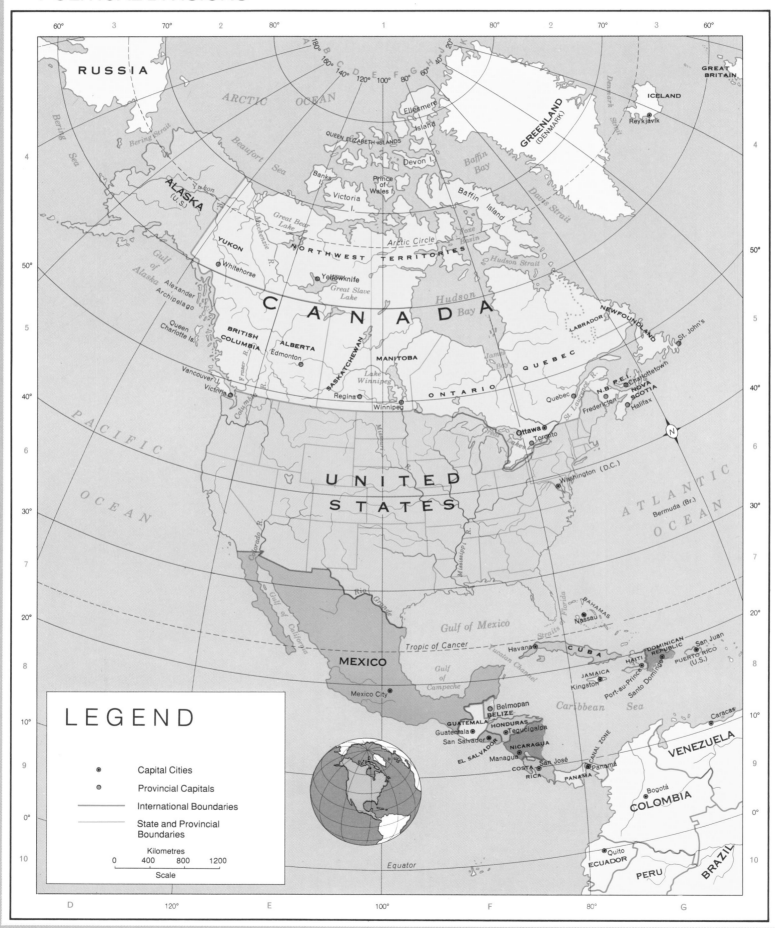

RUSSIA

ARCTIC OCEAN

GREAT BRITAIN

ICELAND

Reykjavik

GREENLAND
(DENMARK)

Bering Strait

Beaufort Sea

Queen Elizabeth Islands

Devon I.

Ellesmere Island

ALASKA
(U.S.)

Banks I.

Prince of Wales I.

Victoria I.

Baffin Bay

Baffin Island

Davis Strait

Denmark Strait

YUKON

Great Bear Lake

Mackenzie R.

NORTHWEST TERRITORIES

Arctic Circle

Foxe Basin

Whitehorse

Yellowknife

Great Slave Lake

Hudson Strait

Gulf of Alaska

Alexander Archipelago

C A N A D A

Hudson Bay

NEWFOUNDLAND

LABRADOR

Queen Charlotte Is.

BRITISH COLUMBIA

Fraser R.

ALBERTA

SASKATCHEWAN

MANITOBA

James Bay

QUEBEC

St. John's

Edmonton

Lake Winnipeg

Vancouver I.

Victoria

Columbia R.

Regina

Winnipeg

ONTARIO

Quebec

Fredericton

N.B.

P.E.I.

Charlottetown

NOVA SCOTIA

Halifax

PACIFIC OCEAN

Ottawa

Toronto

Great Lakes

St. Lawrence R.

N

U N I T E D
S T A T E S

Missouri R.

Washington (D.C.)

ATLANTIC OCEAN

Bermuda (Br.)

Colorado R.

Rio Grande

Gulf of California

Mississippi R.

Gulf of Mexico

Straits of Florida

Tropic of Cancer

BAHAMAS

Nassau

Yucatan Channel

Havana

C U B A

DOMINICAN REPUBLIC

San Juan

PUERTO RICO
(U.S.)

MEXICO

Gulf of Campeche

JAMAICA

Kingston

HAITI

Port-au-Prince

Santo Domingo

Mexico City

Belmopan

BELIZE

Caribbean Sea

Caracas

GUATEMALA

HONDURAS

Tegucigalpa

Guatemala

San Salvador

EL SALVADOR

NICARAGUA

Managua

CANAL ZONE

VENEZUELA

COSTA RICA

San José

PANAMA

Panama

Bogotá

COLOMBIA

Quito

ECUADOR

PERU

BRAZIL

Equator

LEGEND

- • Capital Cities
- • Provincial Capitals
- —— International Boundaries
- —— State and Provincial Boundaries

Kilometres

0   400   800   1200

Scale

Parliament Buildings, Ottawa

The White House, Washington

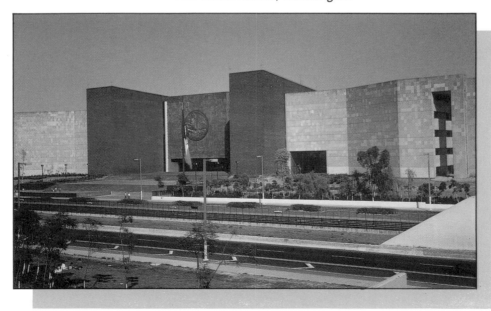

Legislative Buildings, Mexico City

North America
LANDFORMS

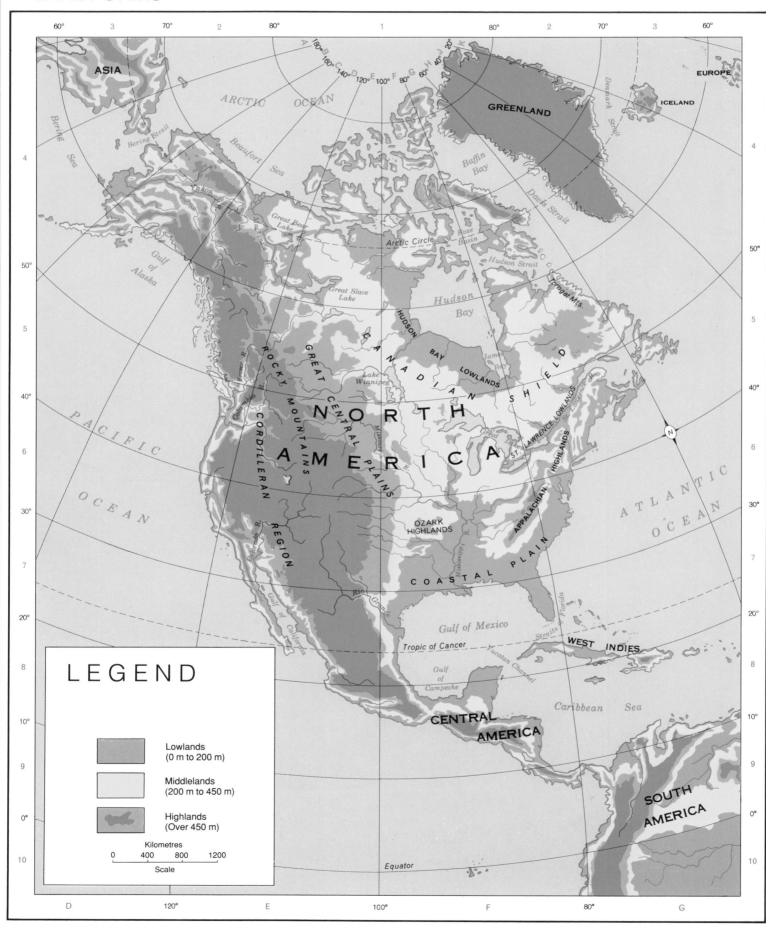

ASIA

ARCTIC OCEAN

Bering Sea

Bering Strait

Beaufort Sea

Yukon R.

Gulf of Alaska

Mackenzie R.

Great Bear Lake

Arctic Circle

Great Slave Lake

GREENLAND

Baffin Bay

Davis Strait

Denmark Strait

ICELAND

EUROPE

Foxe Basin

Hudson Strait

Hudson Bay

James Bay

Torngat Mts.

Peace R.

ROCKY MOUNTAINS

GREAT CENTRAL PLAINS

Fraser R.

Columbia R.

Lake Winnipeg

CANADIAN SHIELD

BAY LOWLANDS

N O R T H

PACIFIC OCEAN

CORDILLERAN REGION

Missouri R.

A M E R I C A

Great Lakes

ST. LAWRENCE LOWLANDS

St. Lawrence R.

HIGHLANDS

APPALACHIAN

ATLANTIC OCEAN

Snake R.

Colorado R.

OZARK HIGHLANDS

Mississippi R.

COASTAL PLAIN

Strait of Florida

Rio Grande

Gulf of California

Gulf of Mexico

Tropic of Cancer

Yucatan Channel

WEST INDIES

Gulf of Campeche

Caribbean Sea

CENTRAL AMERICA

SOUTH AMERICA

Equator

LEGEND

Lowlands (0 m to 200 m)

Middlelands (200 m to 450 m)

Highlands (Over 450 m)

Kilometres
0   400   800   1200
Scale

Gila monster—hot desert animal

Polar bears—cold desert animals

Tundra muskox

Swampland alligator

Grizzly bear—Western North American forest animal

North America
WINTER TEMPERATURES–January Averages

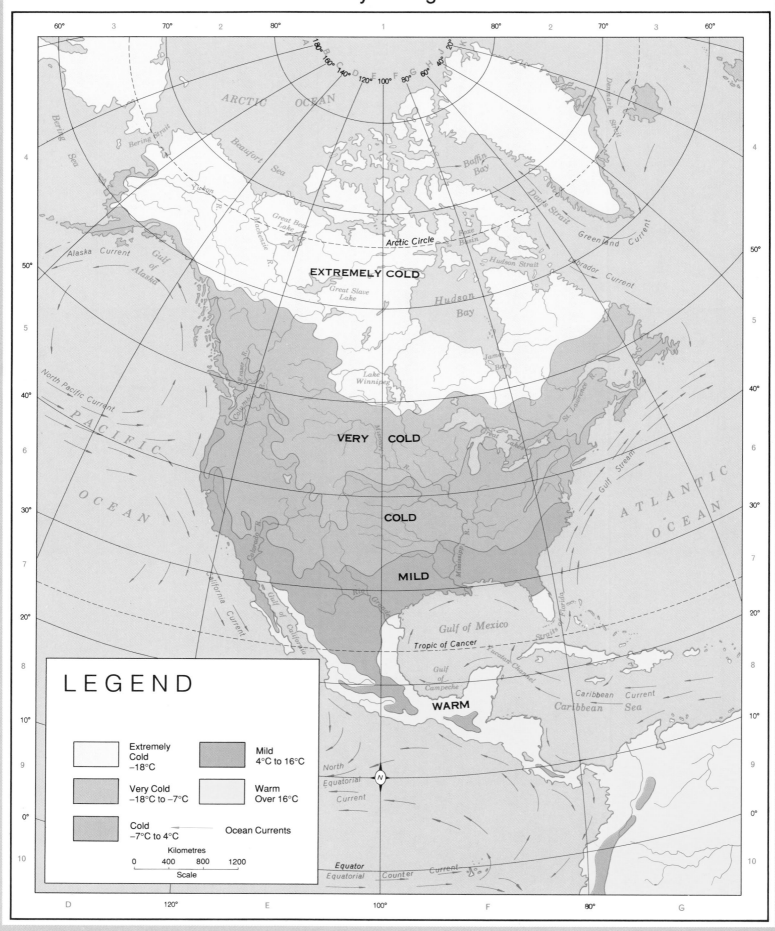

LEGEND

Extremely Cold −18°C	Mild 4°C to 16°C
Very Cold −18°C to −7°C	Warm Over 16°C
Cold −7°C to 4°C	→ Ocean Currents

Kilometres

0   400   800   1200

Scale

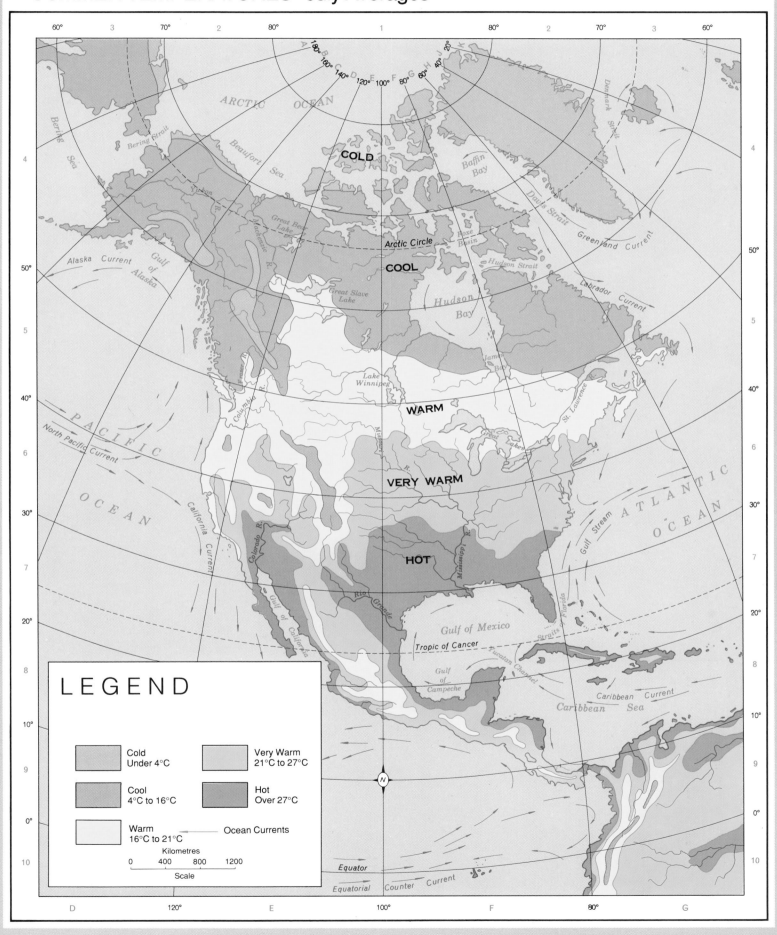

North America
SUMMER TEMPERATURES–July Averages

ARCTIC OCEAN

Bering Strait

Beaufort Sea

COLD

Baffin Bay

Denmark Strait

Alaska Current

Gulf of Alaska

Yukon R.

Great Bear Lake

Mackenzie R.

Arctic Circle

Foxe Basin

Greenland Current

COOL

Great Slave Lake

Hudson Strait

Labrador Current

Hudson Bay

James Bay

Fraser R.

Lake Winnipeg

WARM

St. Lawrence

PACIFIC

North Pacific Current

Columbia R.

Missouri R.

Great Lakes

ATLANTIC OCEAN

OCEAN

VERY WARM

California Current

Colorado R.

HOT

Mississippi R.

Gulf Stream

Rio Grande

Straits of Florida

Gulf of California

Gulf of Mexico

Tropic of Cancer

Yucatan Channel

Gulf of Campeche

Caribbean Current

Caribbean Sea

N

Equator

Equatorial Counter Current

LEGEND

Cold
Under 4°C

Very Warm
21°C to 27°C

Cool
4°C to 16°C

Hot
Over 27°C

Warm
16°C to 21°C

Ocean Currents

Kilometres
0   400   800   1200
Scale

North America
AVERAGE ANNUAL RAINFALL

ARCTIC OCEAN

Bering Sea

Bering Strait

Beaufort Sea

Baffin Bay

Denmark Strait

Yukon

Great Bear Lake

Mackenzie R.

Davis Strait

Arctic Circle

Foxe Basin

Gulf of Alaska

Great Slave Lake

Hudson Strait

Hudson Bay

WESTERLIES

James Bay

PACIFIC

Fraser R.

Columbia R.

Lake Winnipeg

Missouri R.

St. Lawrence R.

Great Lakes

WESTERLIES

OCEAN

Colorado R.

Colorado R.

Mississippi R.

ATLANTIC

OCEAN

N.E. TRADE WINDS

Gulf of California

Rio Grande

Gulf of Mexico

Tropic of Cancer

Straits of Florida

N.E. TRADE WINDS

Gulf of Campeche

Yucatan Channel

Caribbean Sea

N

Equator

LEGEND

	Very Light 0 mm to 250 mm		Heavy 1000 mm to 1500 mm
	Light 250 mm to 500 mm		Very Heavy Over 1500 mm
	Moderate 500 mm to 1000 mm	→	Prevailing Winds

Kilometres

0   400   800   1200

Scale

North America
VEGETATION and LAND USE

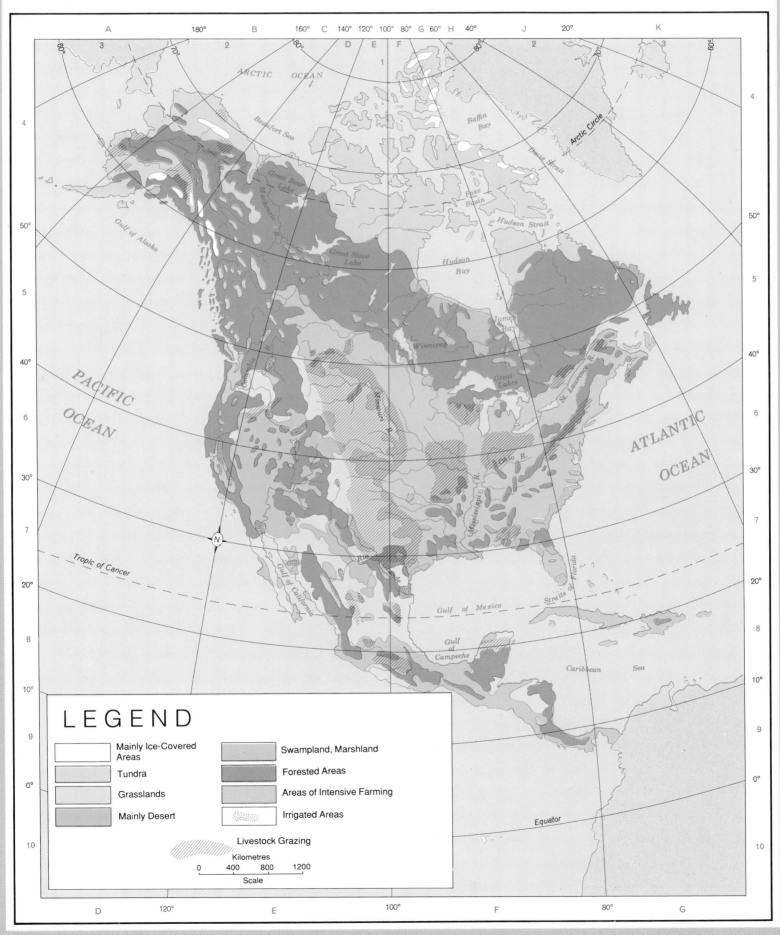

PACIFIC OCEAN

ATLANTIC OCEAN

ARCTIC OCEAN

Beaufort Sea

Baffin Bay

Davis Strait

Arctic Circle

Yukon R.

Great Bear Lake

Mackenzie R.

Foxe Basin

Hudson Strait

Gulf of Alaska

Great Slave Lake

Hudson Bay

James Bay

L. Winnipeg

Columbia R.

Great Lakes

St. Lawrence R.

Missouri R.

Ohio R.

Mississippi R.

Tropic of Cancer

Gulf of California

Straits of Florida

Gulf of Mexico

Gulf of Campeche

Caribbean Sea

Equator

N

LEGEND

Mainly Ice-Covered Areas	Swampland, Marshland
Tundra	Forested Areas
Grasslands	Areas of Intensive Farming
Mainly Desert	Irrigated Areas

Livestock Grazing

Kilometres

0   400   800   1200

Scale

Canada
POLITICAL DIVISIONS

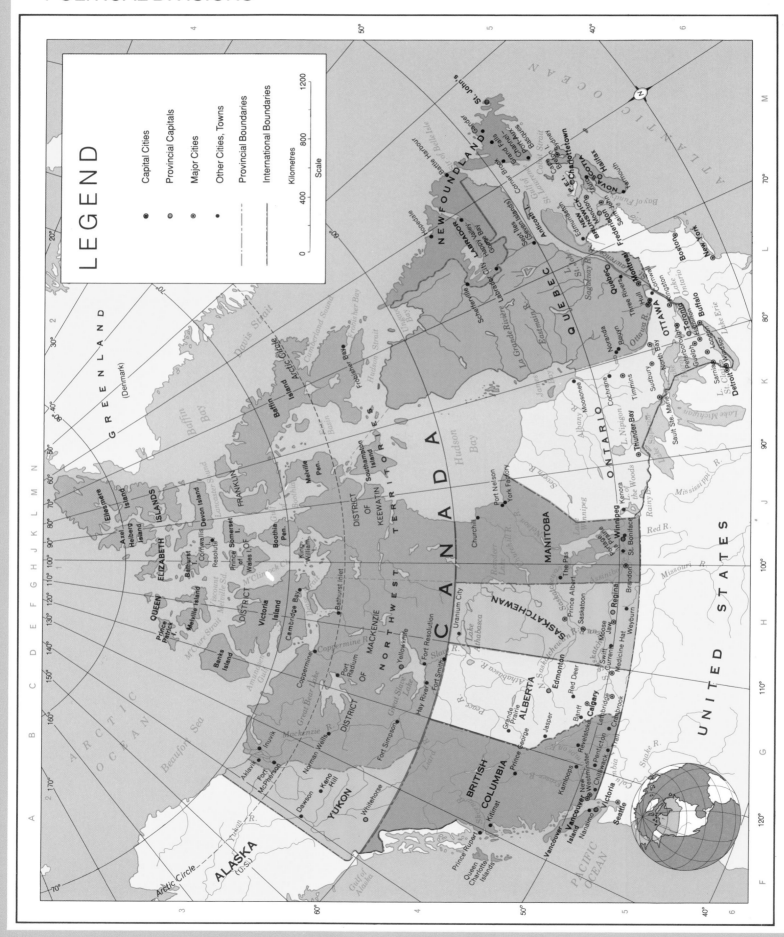

LEGEND

- Capital Cities
- Provincial Capitals
- Major Cities
- Other Cities, Towns
- Provincial Boundaries
- International Boundaries

Kilometres

Scale

0   400   800   1200

Toronto, ON

Halifax, NS

Yellowknife, NWT

St. John's, NF

Charlottetown, PE

Edmonton, AB

Winnipeg, MB

Quebec City, PQ

Regina, SK

Whitehorse, YT

Victoria, BC

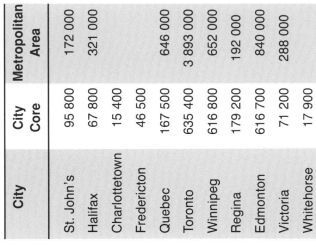

Fredericton, NB

Population of the Capital Cities of Canada

City	City Core	Metropolitan Area
St. John's	95 800	172 000
Halifax	67 800	321 000
Charlottetown	15 400	
Fredericton	46 500	
Quebec	167 500	646 000
Toronto	635 400	3 893 000
Winnipeg	616 800	652 000
Regina	179 200	192 000
Edmonton	616 700	840 000
Victoria	71 200	288 000
Whitehorse	17 900	
Yellowknife	15 200	

Canada
LANDFORMS–Relief

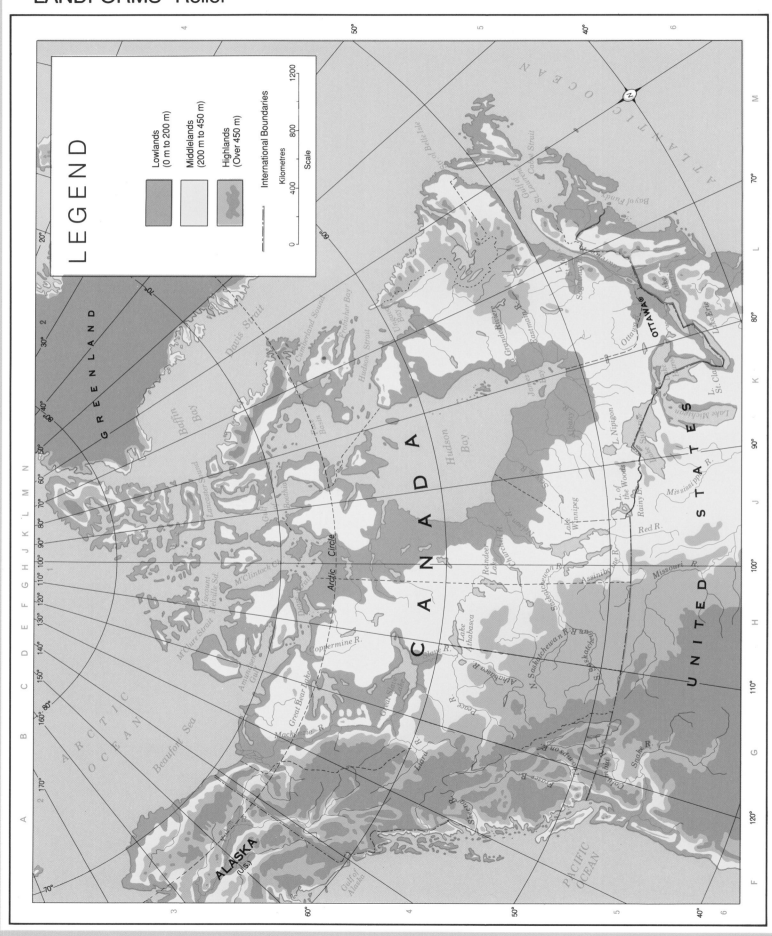

LEGEND

Lowlands (0 m to 200 m)

Middlelands (200 m to 450 m)

Highlands (Over 450 m)

International Boundaries

Scale

Kilometres

Deciduous forest in the fall, ON

Old growth forest, BC

Prairie grasslands, AB

Canada
VEGETATION and LAND–SURFACE REGIONS

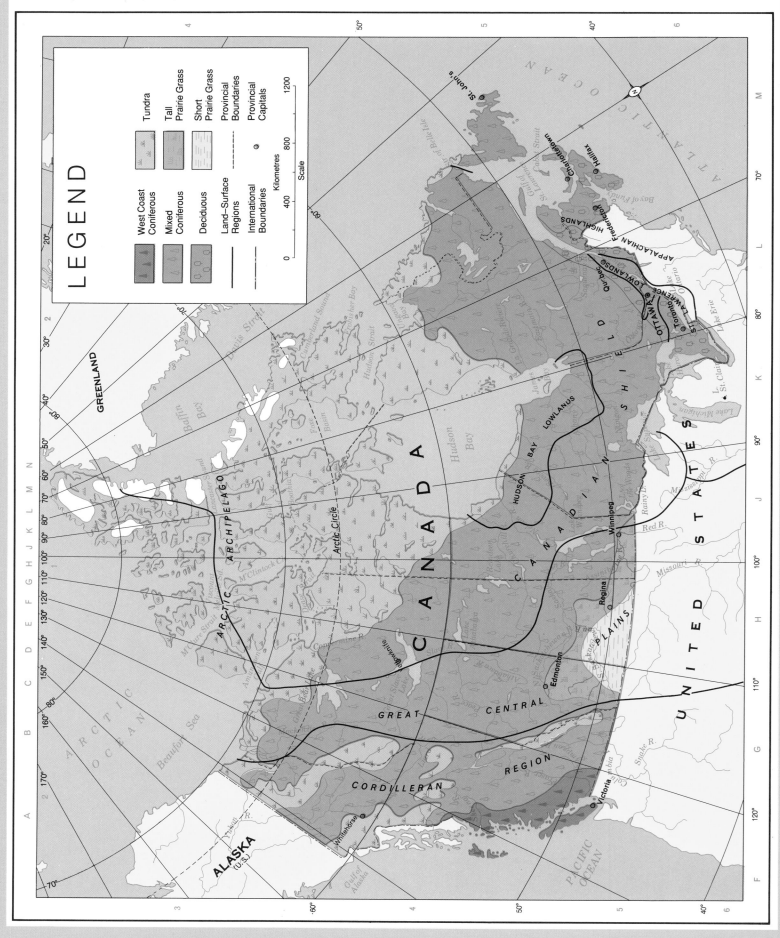

LEGEND

Tundra

Tall Prairie Grass

Short Prairie Grass

Provincial Boundaries

Provincial Capitals

West Coast Coniferous

Mixed Coniferous

Deciduous

Land–Surface Regions

International Boundaries

Scale

Kilometres

0   400   800   1200

Canada
SETTLED AREAS–Population

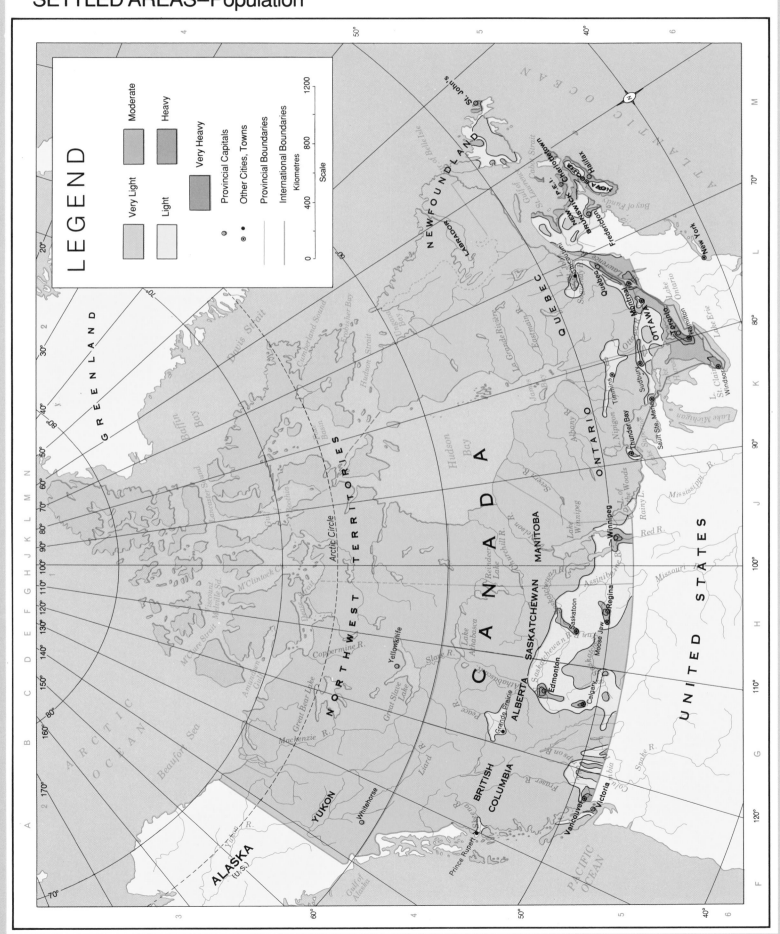

Canada
A MULTICULTURAL SOCIETY

Canadian students

Ukrainians in western Canada

National Backgrounds of Canadians
1991 Census

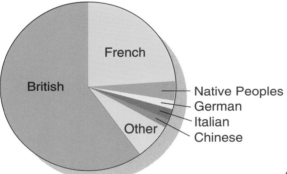

French

British

Native Peoples
German
Italian
Chinese

Other

Bonhomme in Quebec

Ovide Mercredi, national Chief of the Assembly of First Nations, receives the sacred bundle from elder during swearing-in ceremony, June 12, 1991.

Immigration by Province

	Total Immigrants	NF	PE	NS	NB	PQ	ON	MB	SK	AB	BC	YT and NWT
1961	71 689	365	69	901	770	16 920	36 518	2 527	1 333	4 823	7 326	137
1966	194 743	805	141	2 084	1 283	39 198	107 621	5 132	3 440	10 078	24 746	215
1971	121 900	819	172	1 812	1 038	19 222	64 357	5 301	1 426	8 653	18 917	183
1976	149 429	725	235	1 942	1 752	29 282	72 031	5 509	2 323	14 896	20 484	250
1981	128 618	483	128	1 405	990	21 182	55 032	5 370	2 402	19 330	22 095	201
1986	99 219	274	168	1 097	641	19 459	49 630	3 749	1 860	9 673	12 552	116
1991	232 020	641	150	1 504	685	52 155	119 257	5 659	2 455	17 043	32 263	208
1992	253 345	787	151	2 359	754	48 597	138 453	5 084	2 511	17 696	36 709	244
1993	254 663	805	170	3 001	705	44 737	133 665	4 882	2 391	18 487	45 546	274

What do you think attracts newcomers to settle in your province?

East Indian woman displaying traditional cuisine

Kensington Market, Toronto

Caribana Parade in Toronto

Chinatown, Vancouver

Where do immigrants to Canada come from?
(1993)

Europe 18.2
Africa 6.6
Caribbean 6.5
United States 6.2
South America 3.8
Australasia 1.2
Asia 57.5

= 100%

Immigration & Emigration to 1993

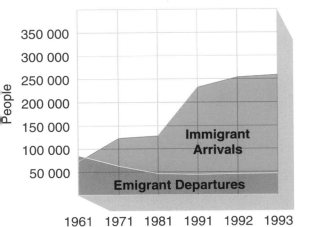

People

350 000
300 000
250 000
200 000
150 000
100 000
50 000

Immigrant Arrivals

Emigrant Departures

1961 1971 1981 1991 1992 1993

Where do refugees to Canada come from?
(1993)

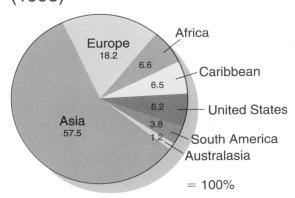

Asia	14 664
Africa	5 173
Eastern Europe	3 642
Central America	3 506
Australasia	2 322
South America	811
Other	52

Total number of people = 30 170

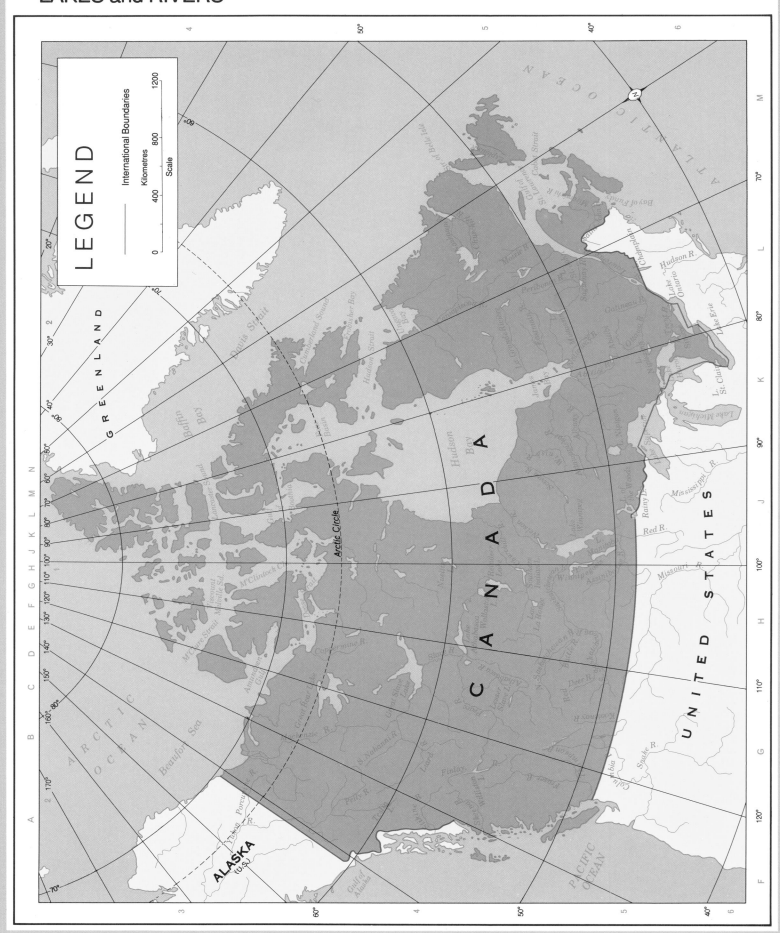

Canada
LAKES and RIVERS

LEGEND

International Boundaries

Kilometres

Scale

0   400   800   1200

Canada
AIR TRANSPORTATION

LEGEND

Principal Air Routes
(Including routes to northland
by smaller companies)

Capital Cities
Provincial Capitals
Major Cities
Other Cities, Towns
Provincial Boundaries
International Boundaries

Kilometres
Scale

0   400   800   1200

Canada
TRANSPORTATION

Competition and rising prices can affect transportation. Canadian railway companies have reorganized services and in some cases cancelled service on existing routes.

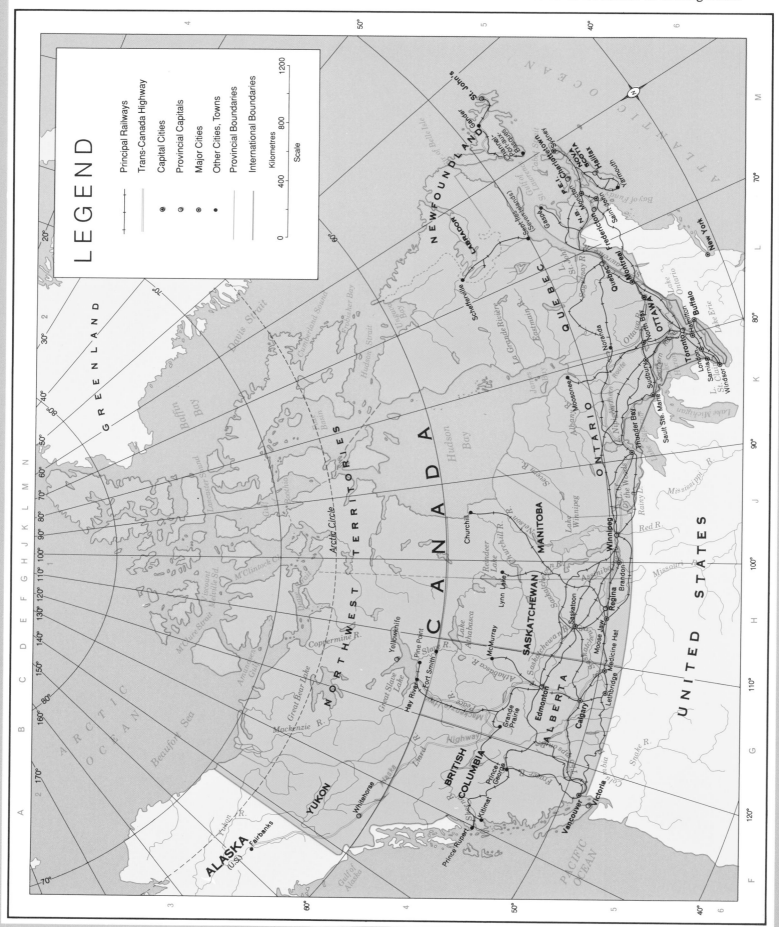

LEGEND

Principal Railways
Trans-Canada Highway
Capital Cities
Provincial Capitals
Major Cities
Other Cities, Towns
Provincial Boundaries
International Boundaries

Kilometres

0   400   800   1200

Scale

Canada
NATURAL RESOURCES

As natural resources are depleted or the demand for them declines, companies close existing mines and seek new sites.

Newfoundland
TRANSPORTATION

Competition and rising prices can affect transportation. Canadian railway companies have reorganized services and in some cases cancelled service on existing routes.

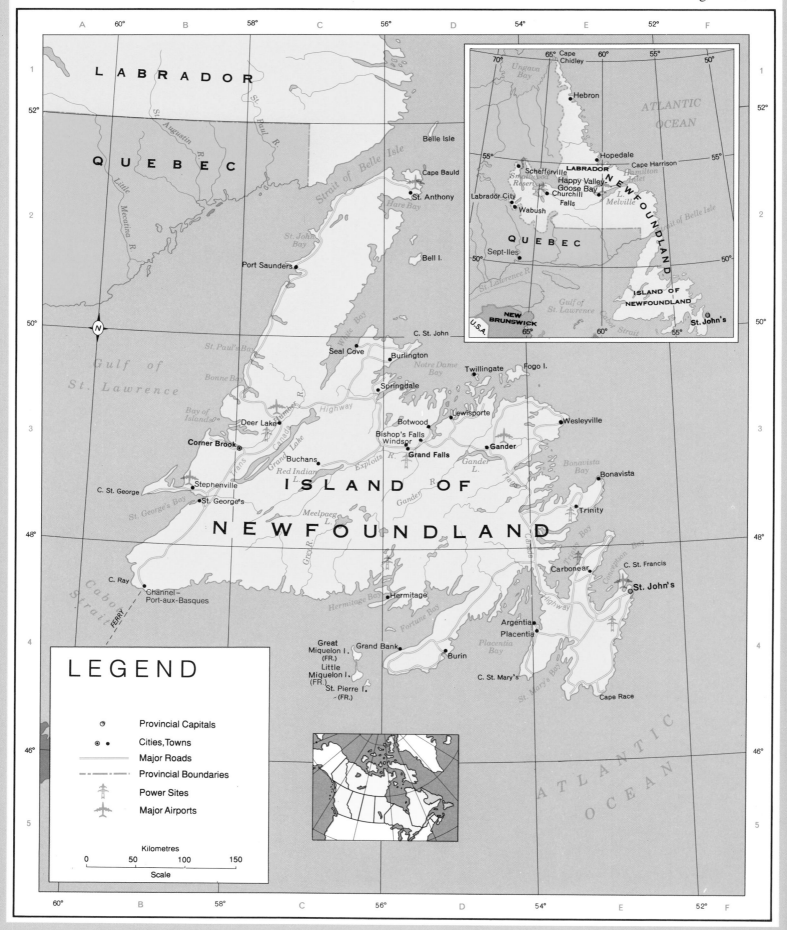

LABRADOR

QUEBEC

St. Augustin R.

St. Paul R.

Little Mecatina R.

Strait of Belle Isle

Belle Isle

Cape Bauld

St. Anthony

Hare Bay

St. John Bay

Port Saunders

Bell I.

Gulf of St. Lawrence

St. Paul's Bay

Bonne Bay

C. St. John

Seal Cove

Burlington

Notre Dame Bay

Twillingate

Fogo I.

Springdale

Bay of Islands

Deer Lake

Humber R.

Highway

Botwood

Lewisporte

Wesleyville

Corner Brook

Canada

Grand Lake

Bishop's Falls
Windsor

Gander

Buchans

Red Indian L.

Exploits R.

Grand Falls

Gander L.

Bonavista Bay

Bonavista

C. St. George

Stephenville

St. George's

ISLAND OF

Gander R.

Trinity

St. George's Bay

Meelpaeg L.

NEWFOUNDLAND

Trinity Bay

C. Ray

Trans

Gros R.

Carbonear

C. St. Francis

Channel–
Port-aux-Basques

FERRY

Conception Bay

St. John's

Cabot Strait

Hermitage Bay

Hermitage

Fortune Bay

Highway

Argentia
Placentia

Great
Miquelon I.
(FR.)

Grand Bank

Burin

Placentia Bay

Little
Miquelon I.
(FR.)

St. Pierre I.
(FR.)

C. St. Mary's

St. Mary's Bay

Cape Race

ATLANTIC OCEAN

Inset map (upper right)

Cape Chidley

Ungava Bay

Hebron

ATLANTIC OCEAN

Hopedale

Cape Harrison

Schefferville

LABRADOR

Smallwood Reservoir

Happy Valley
Goose Bay

Churchill Falls

Hamilton Inlet

L. Melville

Labrador City

NEWFOUNDLAND

Wabush

QUEBEC

Sept-Iles

St. Lawrence R.

Gulf of St. Lawrence

Strait of Belle Isle

NEW BRUNSWICK

U.S.A.

Cabot Strait

ISLAND OF NEWFOUNDLAND

St. John's

LEGEND

- ◉ Provincial Capitals
- ◉ • Cities, Towns
- —— Major Roads
- –·–·– Provincial Boundaries
- ⚡ Power Sites
- ✈ Major Airports

Kilometres

0   50   100   150

Scale

Newfoundland
LANDFORMS–Relief

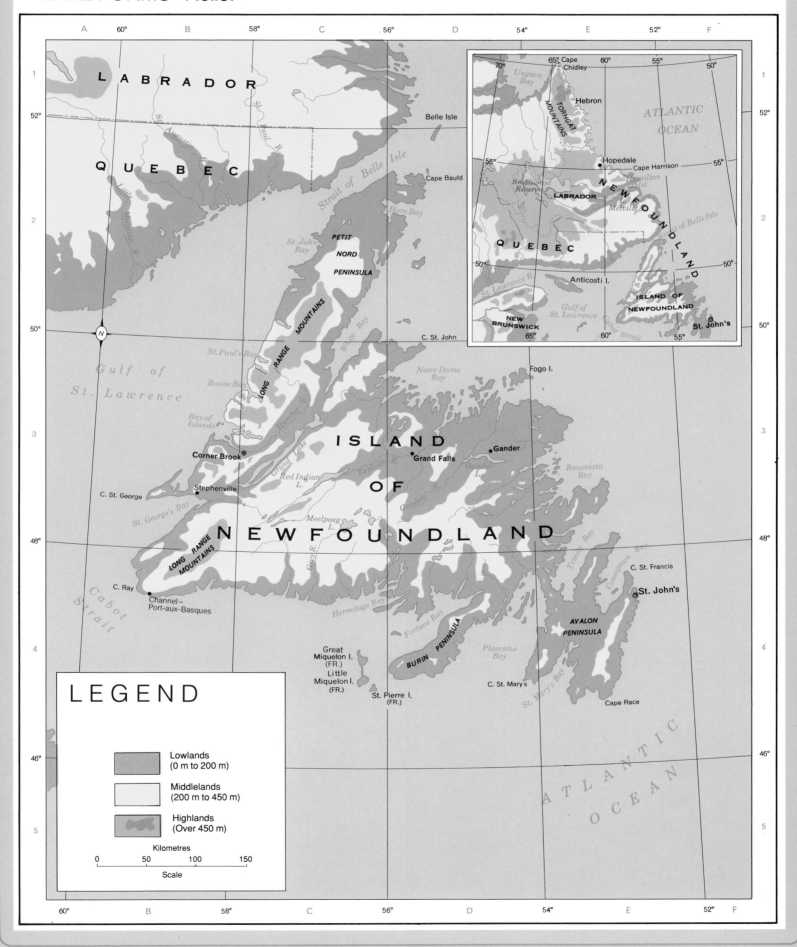

LEGEND

Lowlands
(0 m to 200 m)

Middlelands
(200 m to 450 m)

Highlands
(Over 450 m)

Kilometres

0   50   100   150

Scale

Newfoundland
VEGETATION and INDUSTRIES

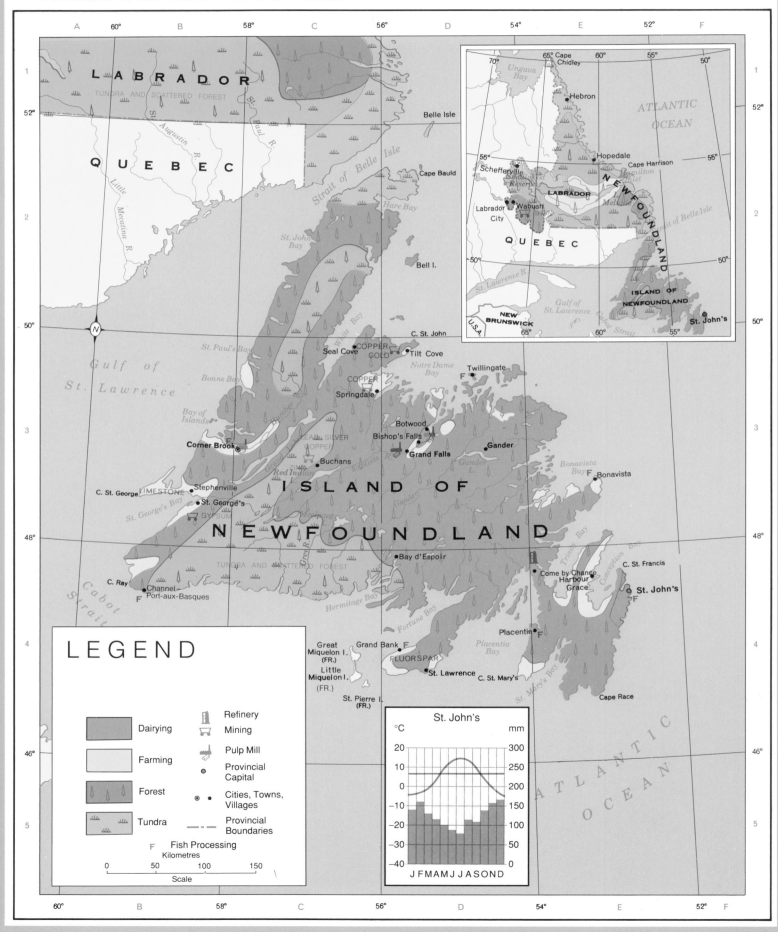

LABRADOR

TUNDRA AND SCATTERED FOREST

QUEBEC

Belle Isle

Cape Bauld

Hare Bay

St. John Bay

Bell I.

Strait of Belle Isle

C. St. John

Seal Cove COPPER GOLD Tilt Cove
Notre Dame Bay
Twillingate
COPPER
Springdale

Gulf of St. Lawrence

St. Paul's Bay

Bonne Bay

Bay of Islands

Botwood
Bishop's Falls
Corner Brook LEAD SILVER COPPER Grand Falls Gander

Buchans

ZINC
Red Indian L.

Bonavista Bay
Bonavista

C. St. George LIMESTONE
Stephenville
St. George's
GYPSUM

ISLAND OF

NEWFOUNDLAND

Bay d'Espoir

Come by Change
Harbour Grace
C. St. Francis

St. John's

C. Ray
Channel Port-aux-Basques

Hermitage Bay

Placentia

Great Miquelon I. (FR.)
Grand Bank
FLUORSPAR
Little Miquelon I. (FR.)
St. Lawrence C. St. Mary's
St. Pierre I. (FR.)

Placentia Bay

Cape Race

ATLANTIC OCEAN

Inset map

Ungava Bay
65° Cape Chidley
Hebron
ATLANTIC OCEAN
Hopedale
Cape Harrison
Schefferville
LABRADOR
NEWFOUNDLAND
Labrador City Wabush
QUEBEC
St. Lawrence R.
Gulf of St. Lawrence
NEW BRUNSWICK
U.S.A.
ISLAND OF NEWFOUNDLAND
St. John's

LEGEND

▨ Dairying	🏭 Refinery
▨ Farming	🏚 Mining
▨ Forest	🏭 Pulp Mill
▨ Tundra	◉ Provincial Capital
	• Cities, Towns, Villages
	–·– Provincial Boundaries

F Fish Processing

Kilometres
0   50   100   150
Scale

St. John's

°C _____ mm
20 _____ 300
10 _____ 250
0 _____ 200
-10 _____ 150
-20 _____ 100
-30 _____ 50
-40 _____ 0
J F M A M J J A S O N D

Maritime Provinces
TRANSPORTATION

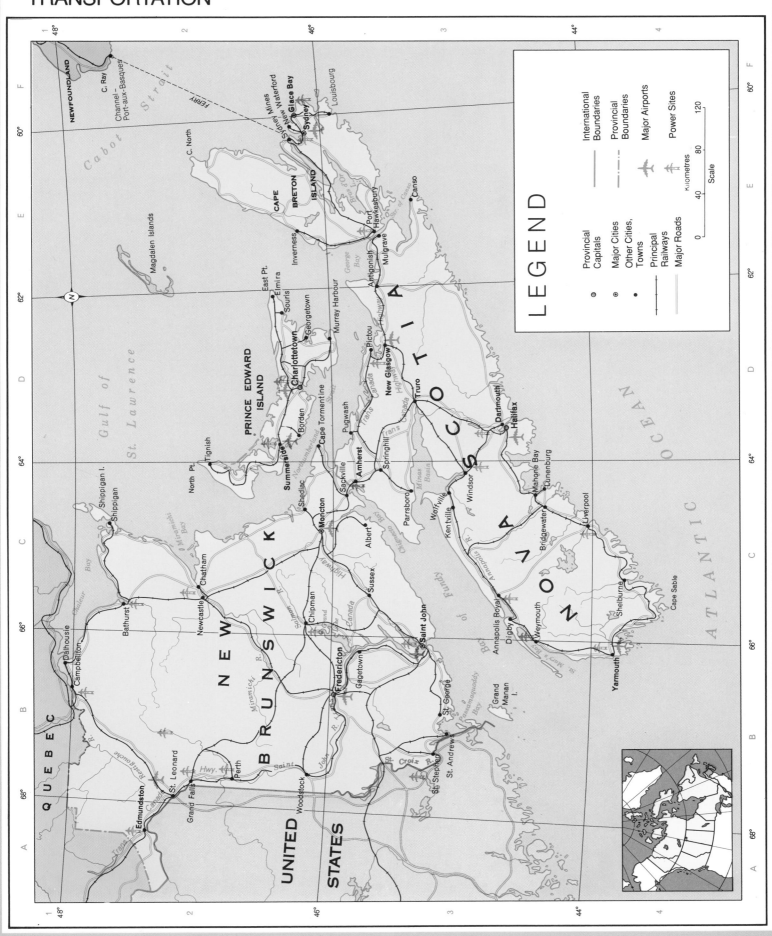

LEGEND

⊙	Provincial Capitals
◎	Major Cities
•	Other Cities, Towns
	Principal Railways
	Major Roads

	International Boundaries
	Provincial Boundaries
✈	Major Airports
✈	Power Sites

Kilometres

0   40   80   120

Scale

QUEBEC

NEWFOUNDLAND

C. Ray

Channel–Port-aux-Basques

Cabot Strait

FERRY

Sydney Mines
New Waterford
Glace Bay
Sydney
Louisbourg

C. North

CAPE BRETON ISLAND

Bras d'Or

Inverness

Magdalen Islands

Gulf of St. Lawrence

Port Hawkesbury
Mulgrave
Str. of Canso
Canso

George Bay

Antigonish

East Pt.
Elmira
Souris

Georgetown
Murray Harbour

PRINCE EDWARD ISLAND

Charlottetown

Pictou
New Glasgow

Summerside
Borden
Cape Tormentine

Northumberland Strait

Truro

Pugwash

Tignish
North Pt.

Trans Canada Highway

Dartmouth
Halifax

Shippigan I.
Shippigan

Shediac
Sackville
Amherst
Springhill

Mahone Bay
Lunenburg

Windsor

NOVA SCOTIA

Chaleur Bay

Bathurst

Moncton

Parrsboro

Minas Basin

Wolfville
Kentville

Liverpool

Miramichi Bay

Chatham
Newcastle

Sussex
Albert

Bay of Fundy

Annapolis R.

Bridgewater

Dalhousie
Campbellton

Miramichi R.

NEW BRUNSWICK

Chipman

Salmon R.

Trans Canada Highway

Digby
Annapolis Royal
Weymouth

Shelburne

Cape Sable

ATLANTIC OCEAN

Restigouche

St. Leonard

Perth

Saint John R.

Fredericton
Gagetown

Saint John

St. George

Grand Manan I.

Passamaquoddy Bay

Yarmouth

St. Mary's Bay

Edmundston
Grand Falls
Woodstock

Hwy.

Trans Canada Hwy.

St. Croix R.
St. Stephen
St. Andrews

UNITED STATES

Maritime Provinces
LANDFORMS—Relief

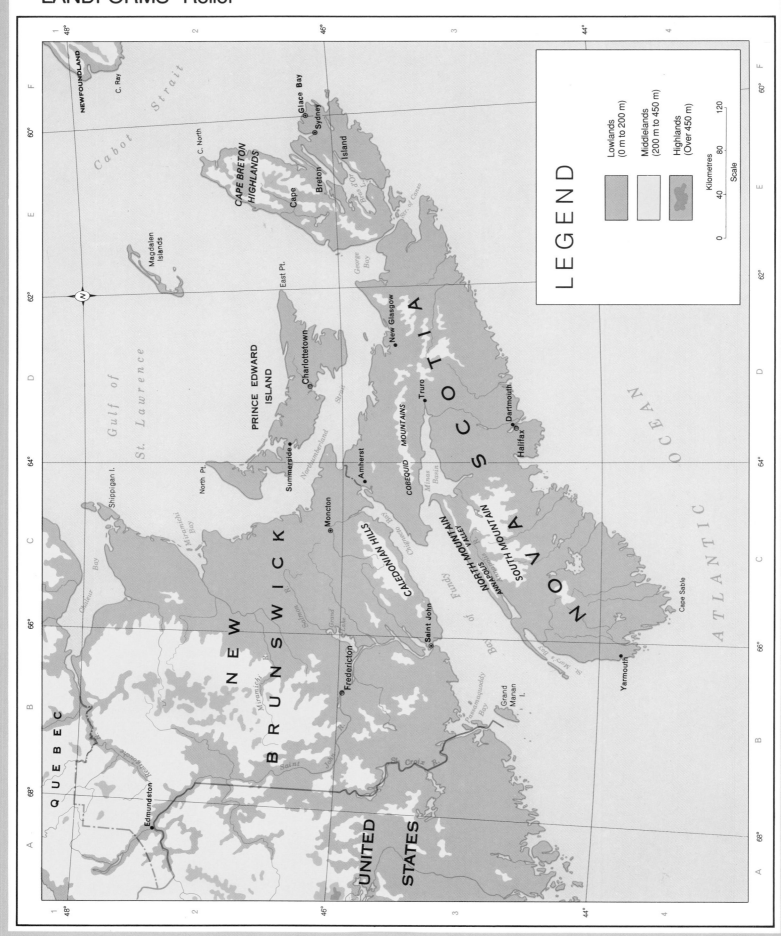

LEGEND

Lowlands (0 m to 200 m)

Middlelands (200 m to 450 m)

Highlands (Over 450 m)

Kilometres

0   40   80   120

Scale

NEWFOUNDLAND

C. Ray

Cabot Strait

C. North

Glace Bay

Sydney

CAPE BRETON HIGHLANDS

Cape Breton Island

Bras d'Or L.

Magdalen Islands

George Bay

East Pt.

Str. of Canso

Gulf of St. Lawrence

New Glasgow

SCOTIA

Charlottetown

PRINCE EDWARD ISLAND

Truro

North Pt.

Northumberland Strait

COBEQUID MOUNTAINS

Dartmouth

Halifax

Shippigan I.

Minas Basin

Summerside

Amherst

Miramichi Bay

NOVA

Chaleur Bay

Chignecto Bay

NORTH MOUNTAIN

Moncton

CALEDONIAN HILLS

ANNAPOLIS VALLEY

SOUTH MOUNTAIN

OCEAN

QUEBEC

Miramichi R.

NEW BRUNSWICK

Grand Lake

Salmon R.

Bay of Fundy

Cape Sable

Saint John

Saint John R.

Fredericton

St. Croix R.

Passamaquoddy Bay

Grand Manan I.

St. Mary's Bay

Yarmouth

ATLANTIC

Restigouche R.

Edmundston

UNITED STATES

Maritime Provinces
FARMING and FORESTRY

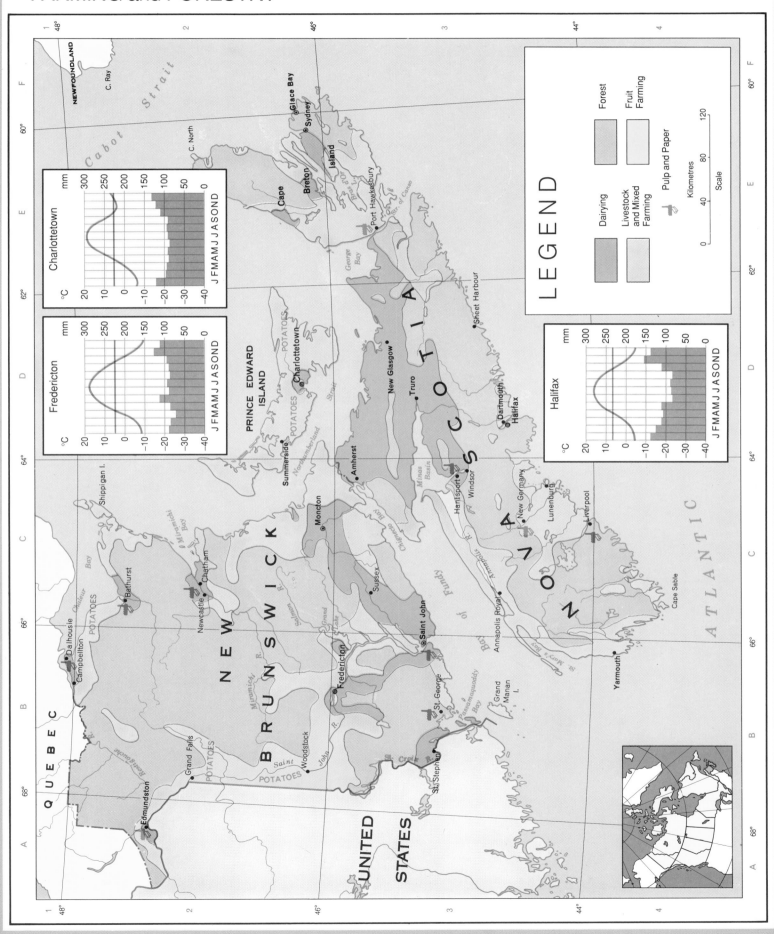

LEGEND

Dairying

Livestock and Mixed Farming

Forest

Fruit Farming

Pulp and Paper

Scale

Kilometres

0 40 80 120

Charlottetown

Fredericton

Halifax

QUEBEC

NEW BRUNSWICK

NOVA SCOTIA

PRINCE EDWARD ISLAND

NEWFOUNDLAND

UNITED STATES

ATLANTIC

Cabot Strait

C. Ray

C. North

Glace Bay
Sydney

Cape Breton Island

Bras d'Or L.

Port Hawkesbury

Str. of Canso

George Bay

Sheet Harbour

Dartmouth
Halifax

New Germany
Lunenburg
Liverpool

Cape Sable

Yarmouth

Annapolis Royal

Bay of Fundy

St. Mary's Bay

Windsor
Hantsport

Minas Basin

Truro
New Glasgow

Amherst

Northumberland Strait

POTATOES

Summerside
Charlottetown

POTATOES

Chignecto Bay

Sussex

Saint John

St. George

Passamaquoddy Bay

Grand Manan I.

St. Croix R.
St. Stephen

Fredericton

Woodstock

POTATOES

Grand Falls

Edmundston

Restigouche

Saint John R.

Grand Lake

Salmon R.

Miramichi R.

Miramichi Bay

Chatham
Newcastle

Bathurst

POTATOES

Chaleur Bay

Dalhousie
Campbellton

Shippigan I.

°C mm
20 300
10 250
0 200
-10 150
-20 100
-30 50
-40 0
J F M A M J J A S O N D

Atlantic Provinces
MINING

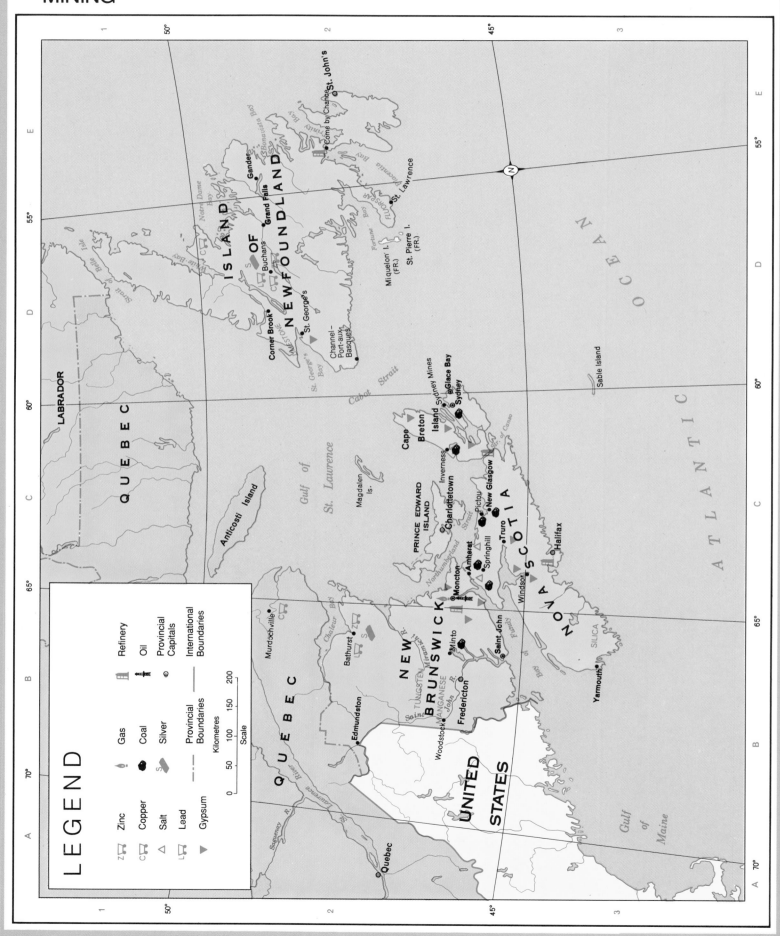

LEGEND

Zinc

Copper

Salt

Lead

Gypsum

Gas

Coal

Silver

Refinery

Oil

Provincial Capitals

International Boundaries

Provincial Boundaries

Scale

Kilometres

0 50 100 150 200

QUEBEC

LABRADOR

ISLAND OF NEWFOUNDLAND

Gander

Grand Falls

Buchans

Corner Brook

St. George's

Channel-Port-aux-Basques

Come by Chance

St. John's

St. Lawrence

Miquelon I. (FR.)

St. Pierre I. (FR.)

Gulf of St. Lawrence

Anticosti Island

Magdalen Is.

Cabot Strait

Cape Breton Island

Sydney Mines

Glace Bay

Sydney

Inverness

PRINCE EDWARD ISLAND

Charlottetown

Pictou

New Glasgow

Truro

NOVA SCOTIA

Halifax

Amherst

Springhill

Moncton

Windsor

Yarmouth

Saint John

Minto

Fredericton

Woodstock

NEW BRUNSWICK

Murdochville

Bathurst

Edmundston

QUEBEC

Quebec

UNITED STATES

ATLANTIC OCEAN

Sable Island

Gulf of Maine

TUNGSTEN

MANGANESE

SILICA

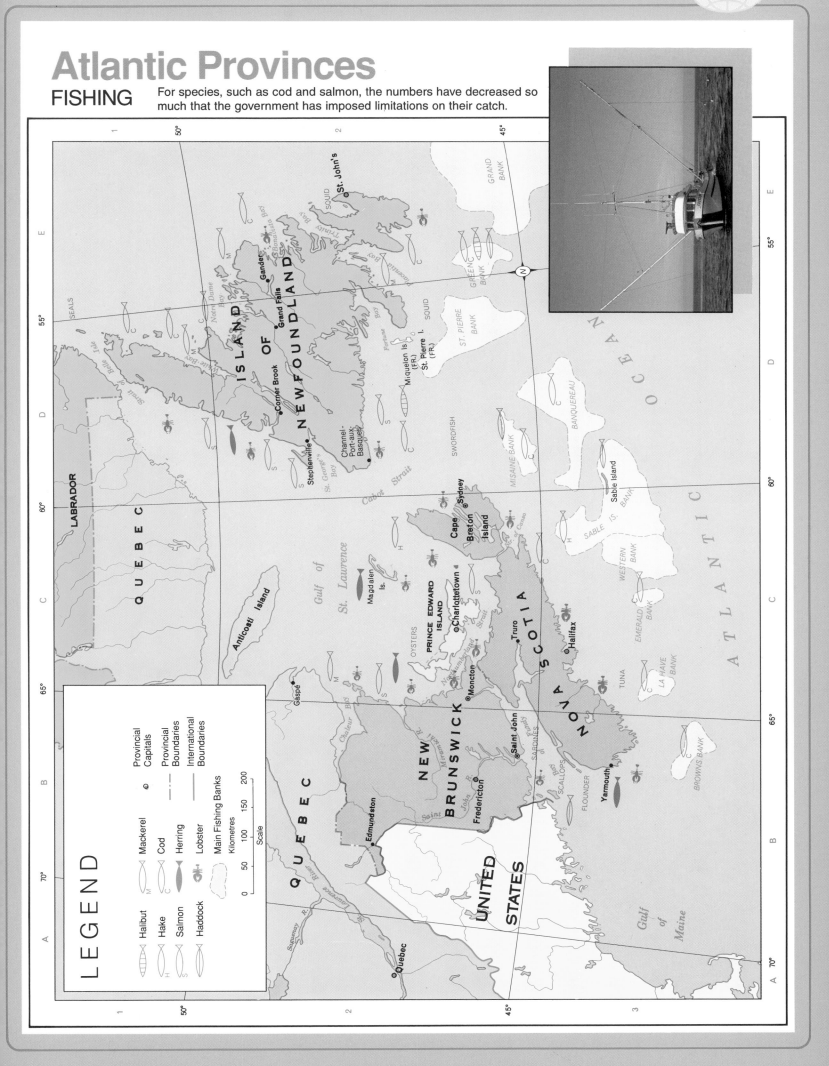

Atlantic Provinces

FISHING For species, such as cod and salmon, the numbers have decreased so much that the government has imposed limitations on their catch.

LEGEND

Halibut
Hake
Salmon
Haddock

Mackerel
Cod
Herring
Lobster

Provincial Capitals
Provincial Boundaries
International Boundaries
Main Fishing Banks

Scale
Kilometres
0 50 100 150 200

QUEBEC
LABRADOR
ISLAND OF NEWFOUNDLAND
St. John's
Gander
Grand Falls
Corner Brook
Stephenville
Channel-Port-aux-Basques
Miquelon Is. (FR.)
St. Pierre I. (FR.)
GRAND BANK
GREEN BANK
ST. PIERRE BANK
NEW BRUNSWICK
NOVA SCOTIA
PRINCE EDWARD ISLAND
Charlottetown
Cape Breton Island
Sydney
Truro
Halifax
Moncton
Saint John
Fredericton
Edmundston
Yarmouth
Gaspé
Anticosti Island
Magdalen Is.
Gulf of St. Lawrence
Cabot Strait
Northumberland Strait
Bay of Fundy
SABLE IS. BANK
Sable Island
BANQUEREAU
MISAINE BANK
WESTERN BANK
EMERALD BANK
LA HAVE BANK
BROWNS BANK
ATLANTIC OCEAN
UNITED STATES
Gulf of Maine
Quebec
St. Lawrence River
Saguenay R.

Quebec
TRANSPORTATION

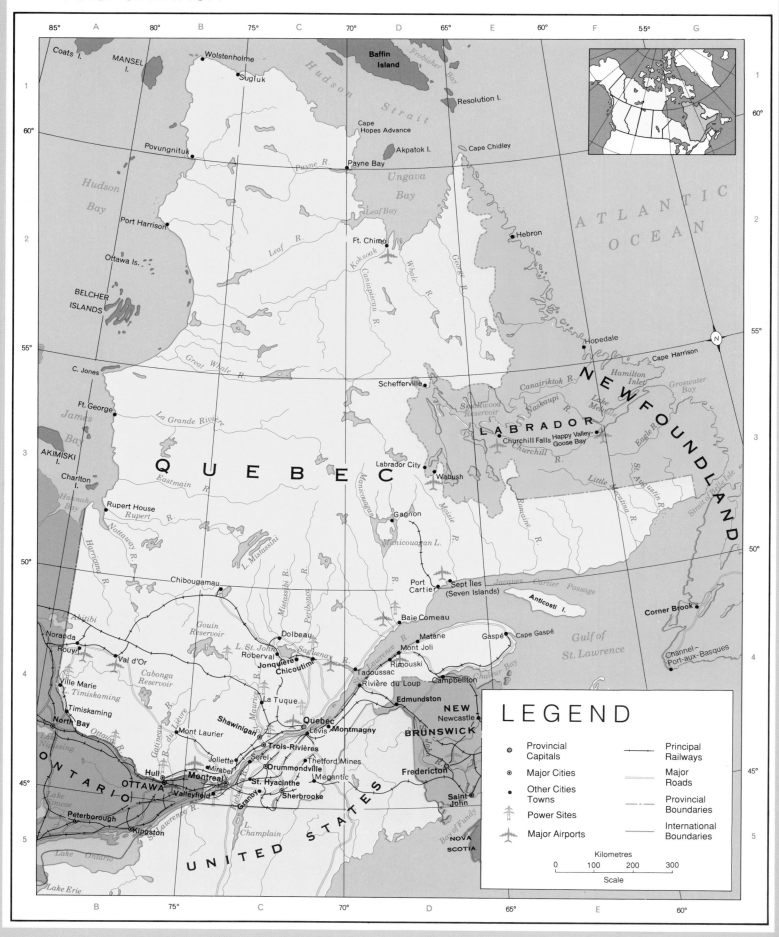

Coats I.

MANSEL I.

Wolstenholme

Sugluk

Baffin Island

Hudson Strait

Frobisher Bay

Resolution I.

Povungnituk

Cape Hopes Advance

Akpatok I.

Cape Chidley

Payne R.

Payne Bay

Hudson Bay

Ungava Bay

Leaf Bay

Leaf R.

Port Harrison

Ottawa Is.

Ft. Chimo

Koksoak R.

Hebron

ATLANTIC OCEAN

BELCHER ISLANDS

Caniapiscau R.

Whale R.

George R.

Great Whale R.

Hopedale

Cape Harrison

C. Jones

Schefferville

NEWFOUNDLAND

Hamilton Inlet

Groswater Bay

Canairiktok R.

Ft. George

James Bay

La Grande Rivière

Smallwood Reservoir

Naskaupi

LABRADOR

Lake Melville

Churchill Falls

Happy Valley Goose Bay

Eagle R.

AKIMISKI I.

Charlton I.

Eastmain R.

QUEBEC

Labrador City

Wabush

Churchill R.

St. Augustin R.

Hannah Bay

Rupert House

Rupert R.

Manicouagan R.

Gagnon

Moisie R.

Romaine R.

Little Mecatina R.

Strait of Belle Isle

Nottaway R.

L. Mistassini

Manicouagan L.

Harricana R.

Chibougamau

Mistassibi R.

Peribonca R.

Port Cartier

Sept Îles (Seven Islands)

Jacques Cartier Passage

Corner Brook

Abitibi

Gouin Reservoir

Dolbeau

Baie Comeau

Anticosti I.

Gulf of St. Lawrence

Channel-Port-aux-Basques

Noranda

Rouyn

Val d'Or

L. St. John

Roberval

Jonquière

Chicoutimi

Saguenay R.

Matane

Mont Joli

Gaspé

Cape Gaspé

Cabonga Reservoir

Ville Marie

L. Timiskaming

Tadoussac

Rimouski

St. Lawrence

Timiskaming

La Tuque

Rivière du Loup

Campbellton

Chaleur Bay

North Bay

Maurice R.

Shawinigan

Edmundston

NEW

Lake Nipissing

Mont Laurier

Quebec

Lévis

Montmagny

Newcastle

BRUNSWICK

Gatineau R.

Joliette

Trois-Rivières

Thetford Mines

R. du Lièvre

Mirabel

Sorel

Drummondville

Mégantic

Fredericton

St. John R.

ONTARIO

Hull

OTTAWA

Montreal

St. Hyacinthe

Saint John

Lake Simcoe

Valleyfield

Granby

Sherbrooke

UNITED STATES

Peterborough

Kingston

St. Lawrence R.

L. Champlain

Bay of Fundy

NOVA SCOTIA

Lake Ontario

Lake Erie

LEGEND

⊙ Provincial Capitals		┼ Principal Railways
⊚ Major Cities		═ Major Roads
● Other Cities Towns		─ ─ Provincial Boundaries
⌁ Power Sites		── International Boundaries
✈ Major Airports		

Kilometres

0   100   200   300

Scale

Quebec
LANDFORMS–Relief

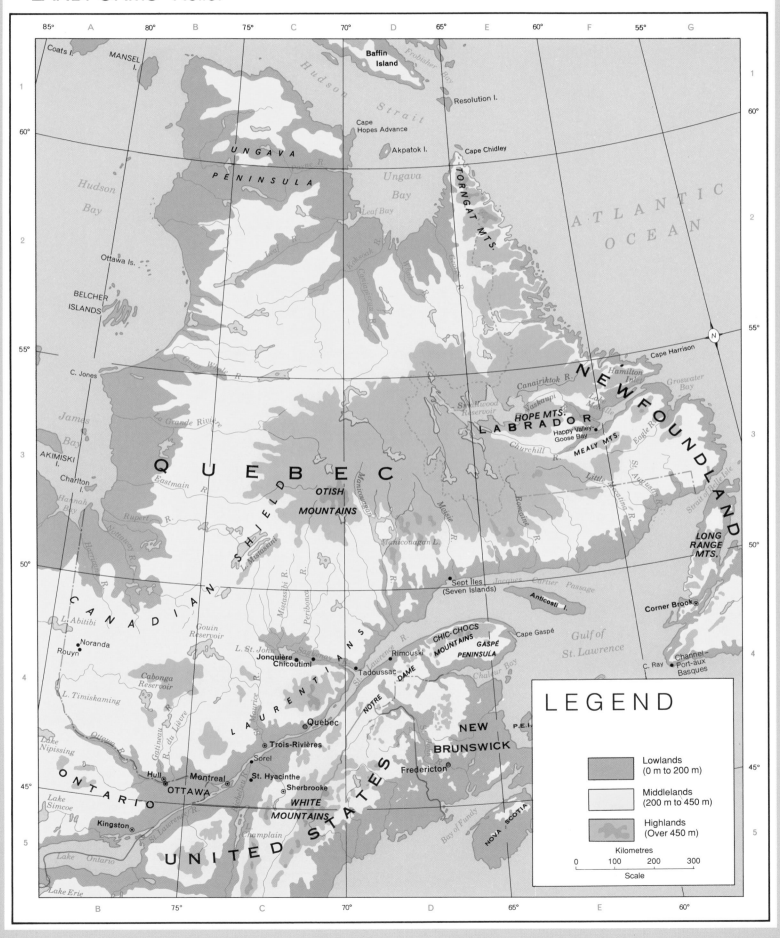

Coats I.
MANSEL I.
Baffin Island
Frobisher Bay
Hudson Strait
Resolution I.
Cape Hopes Advance
UNGAVA PENINSULA
Akpatok I.
Cape Chidley
Ungava Bay
Hudson Bay
Leaf Bay
Leaf R.
Povungnituk R.
TORNGAT MTS.
ATLANTIC OCEAN
Ottawa Is.
BELCHER ISLANDS
C. Jones
Koksoak R.
Caniapiscau R.
N
Cape Harrison
Canairiktok R.
Hamilton Inlet
Groswater Bay
James Bay
Great Whale R.
La Grande Rivière
Smallwood Reservoir
Naskaupi
HOPE MTS.
LABRADOR
NEWFOUNDLAND
Happy Valley Goose Bay
Lake Melville
AKIMISKI I.
Charlton I.
Eastmain R.
QUEBEC
OTISH MOUNTAINS
Churchill R.
MEALY MTS.
Eagle R.
Hannah Bay
Rupert R.
Manicouagan R.
Little Mecatina R.
St. Augustin R.
Strait of Belle Isle
Nottaway R.
Mistassini
SHIELD
Moisie R.
Romaine R.
Harricana R.
L. Mistassini
Mistassibi R.
Peribonca R.
Manicouagan L.
LONG RANGE MTS.
CANADIAN
L. Abitibi
Gouin Reservoir
Sept Îles (Seven Islands)
Jacques Cartier Passage
Anticosti I.
Corner Brook
Noranda
Rouyn
Cabonga Reservoir
L. Timiskaming
L. St. John
Jonquière
Chicoutimi
Saguenay R.
LAURENTIANS
Tadoussac
St. Lawrence R.
Rimouski
CHIC-CHOCS MOUNTAINS
GASPÉ PENINSULA
Cape Gaspé
Gulf of St. Lawrence
C. Ray
Channel-Port-aux Basques
Lake Nipissing
Lièvre R.
Gatineau R.
Lachelle R.
Quebec
NOTRE DAME
Chaleur Bay
NEW BRUNSWICK
P.E.I.
Trois-Rivières
Sorel
ONTARIO
Hull
OTTAWA
Montreal
St. Hyacinthe
Sherbrooke
Fredericton
UNITED STATES
Lake Simcoe
Kingston
WHITE MOUNTAINS
Champlain
Bay of Fundy
NOVA SCOTIA
Lake Ontario
Lake Erie
Ottawa R.
St. Lawrence R.

LEGEND

Lowlands (0 m to 200 m)

Middlelands (200 m to 450 m)

Highlands (Over 450 m)

Kilometres
0   100   200   300
Scale

Quebec
MINING

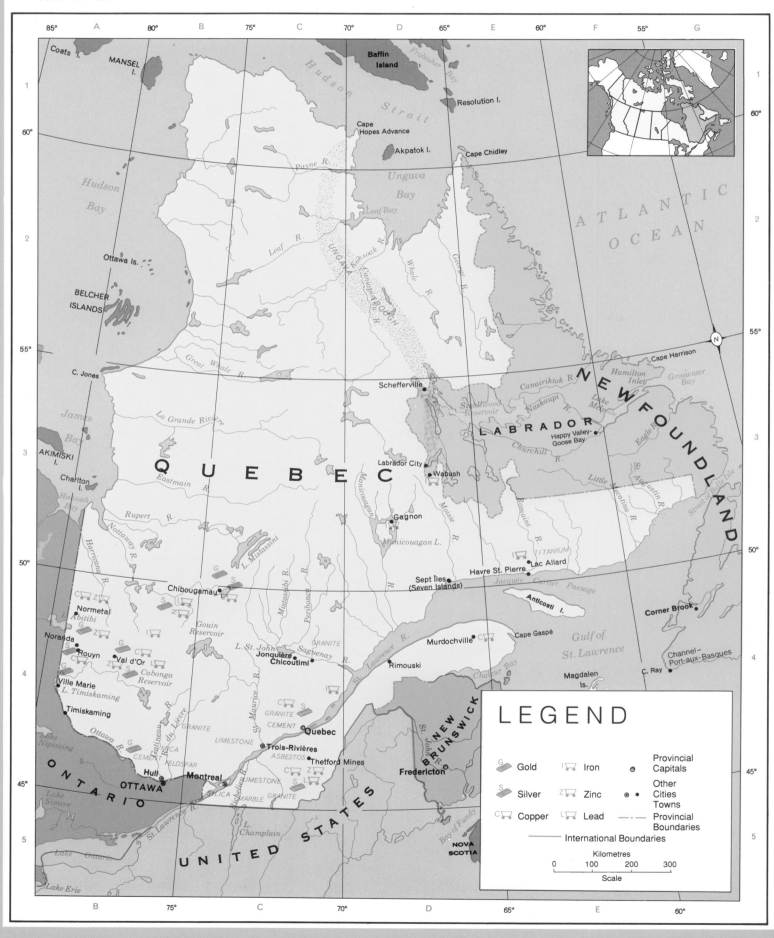

LEGEND

- Gold
- Silver
- Copper
- Iron
- Zinc
- Lead
- Provincial Capitals
- Other Cities Towns
- Provincial Boundaries
- International Boundaries

Kilometres
0   100   200   300
Scale

Quebec
FARMING and INDUSTRIES

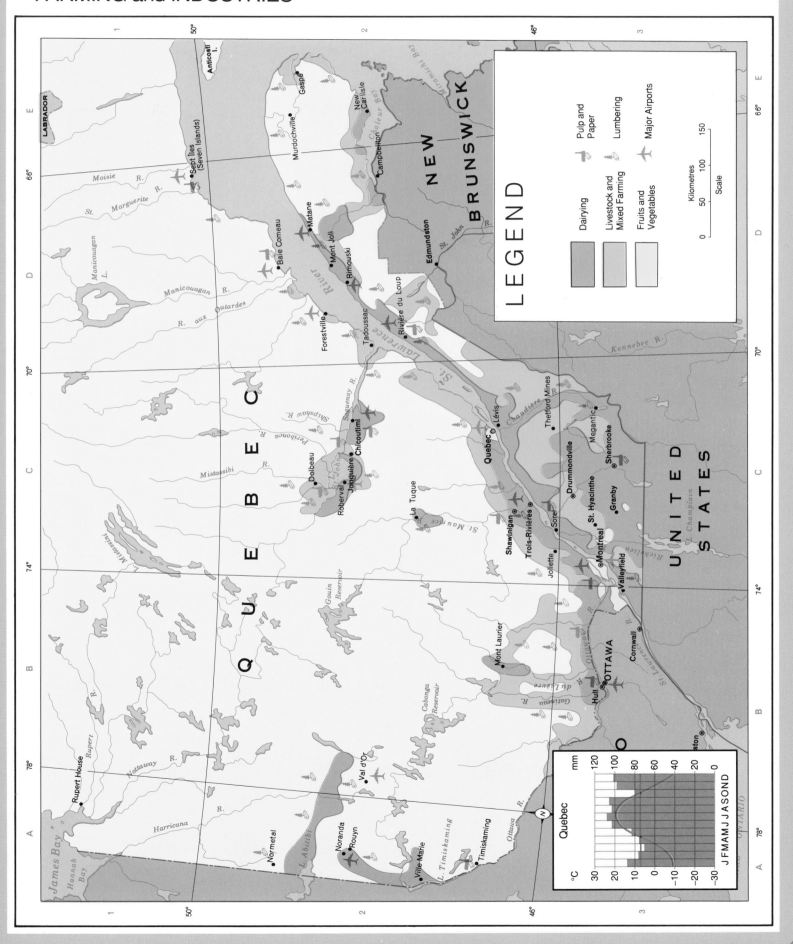

LABRADOR

Anticosti I.

Gaspé

New Carlisle

Murdochville

Campbellton

Chaleur Bay

NEW

BRUNSWICK

Matane

Baie Comeau

Mont Joli

Rimouski

Edmundston

Sept Îles (Seven Islands)

Moisie R.

St. Marguerite R.

Manicouagan L.

Manicouagan R.

R. aux Outardes

Forestville

Tadoussac

Rivière du Loup

St. John

Q

U

E

B

E

C

Saguenay R.

Shipshaw R.

Péribonca R.

Mistassibi R.

Lake St. John

Dolbeau

Roberval

Jonquière

Chicoutimi

La Tuque

St. Maurice R.

Lévis

Quebec

Chaudière R.

Thetford Mines

Mégantic

Sherbrooke

Granby

Drummondville

St. Hyacinthe

Shawinigan

Trois-Rivières

Sorel

Joliette

Montréal

Valleyfield

L. Champlain

Richelieu R.

U **N** **I** **T** **E** **D**

S **T** **A** **T** **E** **S**

Kennebec R.

Kamouraska

Mistassini L.

Gouin Reservoir

Mont Laurier

Cabonga Reservoir

Gatineau R.

R. du Lièvre

OTTAWA

Hull

Cornwall

St. Lawrence

ONTARIO

Ottawa R.

Rupert House

Rupert R.

Nottaway R.

Harricana R.

James Bay

Hannah Bay

Normetal

Noranda

Rouyn

L. Abitibi

Val d'Or

Ville-Marie

Timiskaming

L. Timiskaming

LEGEND

Dairying	Pulp and Paper
Livestock and Mixed Farming	Lumbering
Fruits and Vegetables	Major Airports

Kilometres

0   50   100   150

Scale

Quebec

°C   mm

30   120

      100

20   80

10   60

0   40

-10   20

-20   0

-30

J F M A M J J A S O N D

N

Southern Ontario
TRANSPORTATION

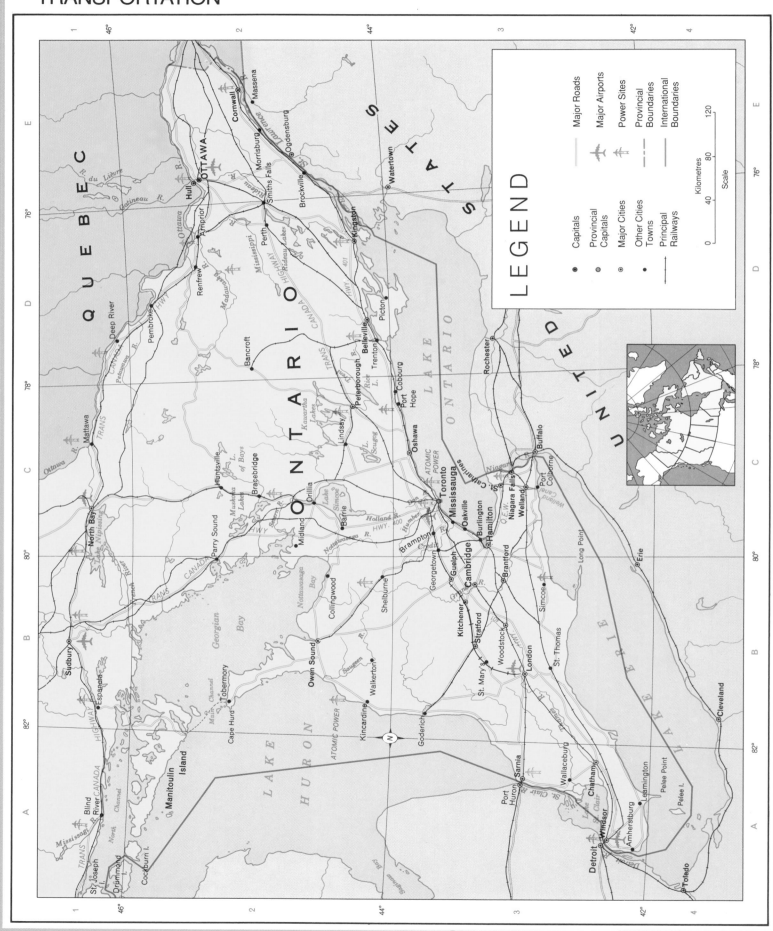

LEGEND

Capitals
Provincial Capitals
Major Cities
Other Cities Towns
Principal Railways

Major Roads
Major Airports
Power Sites
Provincial Boundaries
International Boundaries

Scale
Kilometres
0   40   80   120

Southern Ontario
LANDFORMS–Relief

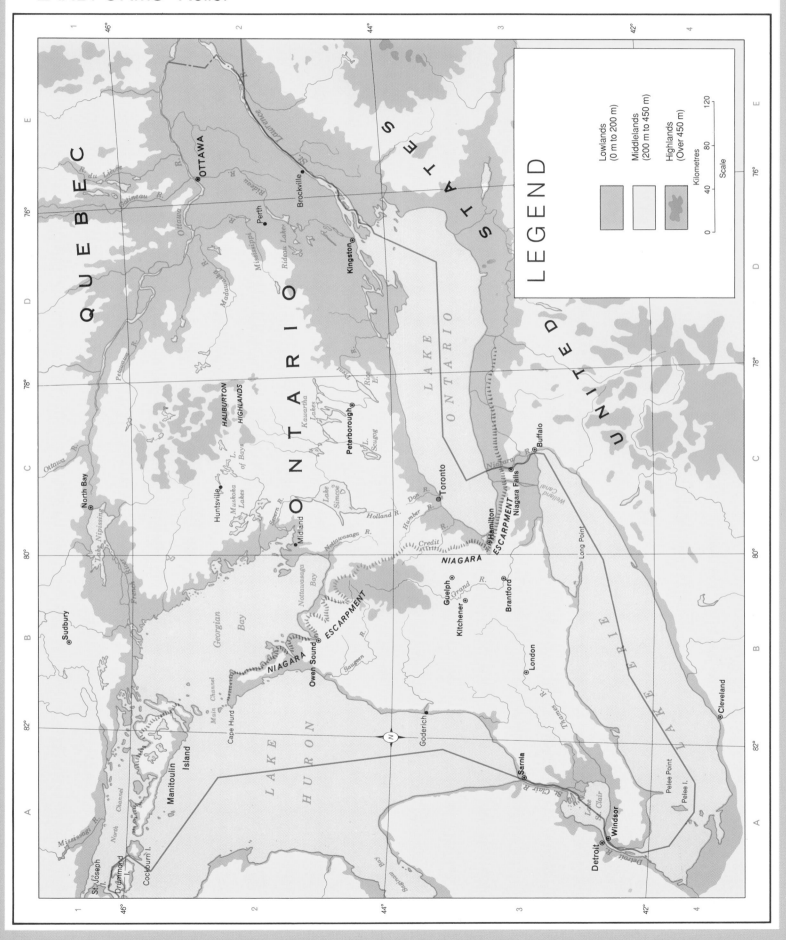

LEGEND

Lowlands (0 m to 200 m)

Middlelands (200 m to 450 m)

Highlands (Over 450 m)

Scale

Kilometres

0   40   80   120

Southern Ontario
FARMING

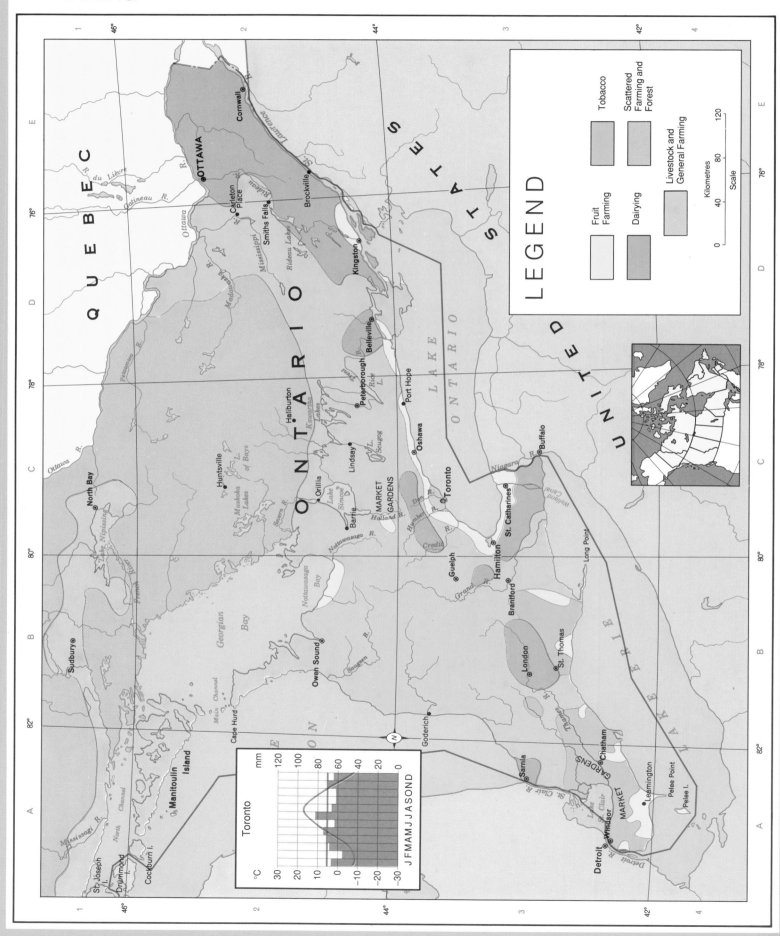

LEGEND

Fruit Farming

Tobacco

Dairying

Scattered Farming and Forest

Livestock and General Farming

Scale

Kilometres

0   40   80   120

Toronto

QUEBEC

ONTARIO

UNITED STATES

LAKE ONTARIO

LAKE ERIE

LAKE HURON

Georgian Bay

Ottawa
Cornwall
Carleton Place
Smiths Falls
Brockville
Kingston
Belleville
Peterborough
Port Hope
Haliburton
Lindsay
Oshawa
Toronto
Orillia
Barrie
MARKET GARDENS
St. Catharines
Niagara
Buffalo
Guelph
Hamilton
Brantford
London
St. Thomas
Long Point
Goderich
Sarnia
Chatham
MARKET GARDENS
Leamington
Pelee Point
Pelee I.
Windsor
Detroit
Huntsville
North Bay
Sudbury
Owen Sound
Cape Hurd
Manitoulin Island
St. Joseph I.
Drummond I.
Cockburn I.

Southern Ontario
MINING and INDUSTRIES

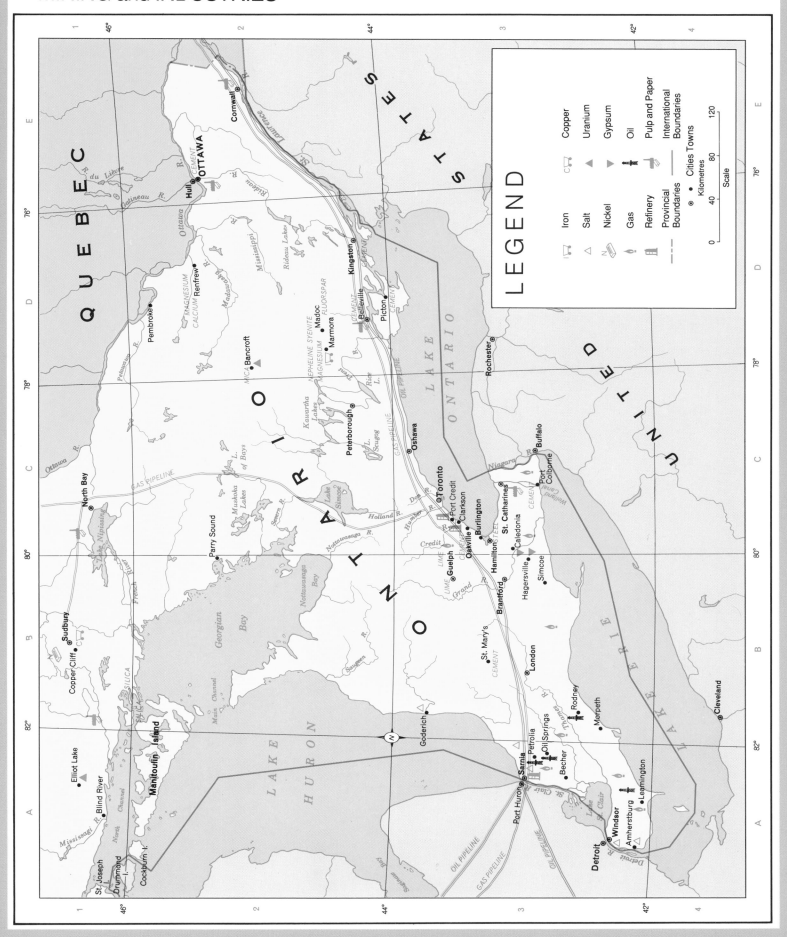

LEGEND

Iron	Copper		
Salt	Uranium		
Nickel	Gypsum		
Gas	Oil		
Refinery	Pulp and Paper		
Provincial Boundaries	International Boundaries		
Cities Towns			

Scale
Kilometres
0   40   80   120

QUEBEC

QUÉBEC

UNITED STATES

UNITED STATES

ONTARIO

LAKE ONTARIO

LAKE ERIE

LAKE HURON

Georgian Bay

Lake Nipissing

R. du Lièvre
Gatineau R.
Ottawa R.
Mississippi R.
Rideau Lakes
Madawaska R.
Petawawa R.
Bonnechere R.
Mississippi R.
Rideau R.
St. Lawrence R.
Kawartha Lakes
L. of Bays
Muskoka Lakes
Scugog L.
Rice L.
Trent R.
Otonabee R.
Lake Simcoe
Holland R.
Nottawasaga R.
Severn R.
Don R.
Humber R.
Credit R.
Grand R.
Thames R.
Saugeen R.
Maitland R.
French River
Spanish River
North Channel
Mississagi R.
St. Clair R.
Detroit R.
Lake St. Clair
Welland Canal
Niagara R.
Nottawasaga Bay

Cornwall
Ottawa OTTAWA CEMENT
Hull CEMENT
Renfrew MAGNESIUM CALCIUM
Pembroke
Bancroft MICA
Kingston CEMENT
Belleville CEMENT
Picton CEMENT
Madoc FLUORSPAR
Marmora
Peterborough
NEPHELINE SYENITE
MAGNESIUM
North Bay
Parry Sound
Oshawa
Toronto
Port Credit
Clarkson
Oakville
Burlington CEMENT
Hamilton STEEL
St. Catharines
Caledonia
Simcoe
Hagersville
Port Colborne CEMENT
Buffalo
Rochester
Guelph LIME
Brantford
St. Mary's CEMENT
London
Goderich
Sarnia
Petrolia
Oil Springs
Becher
Rodney
Morpeth
Leamington
Windsor
Amherstburg
Detroit
Port Huron
Cleveland
Sudbury
Copper Cliff
Elliot Lake
Blind River
St. Joseph I.
Drummond I.
Cockburn I.
Manitoulin Island
SILICA
GAS PIPELINE
OIL PIPELINE
GAS PIPELINE
OIL PIPELINE
N

Northern Ontario
TRANSPORTATION

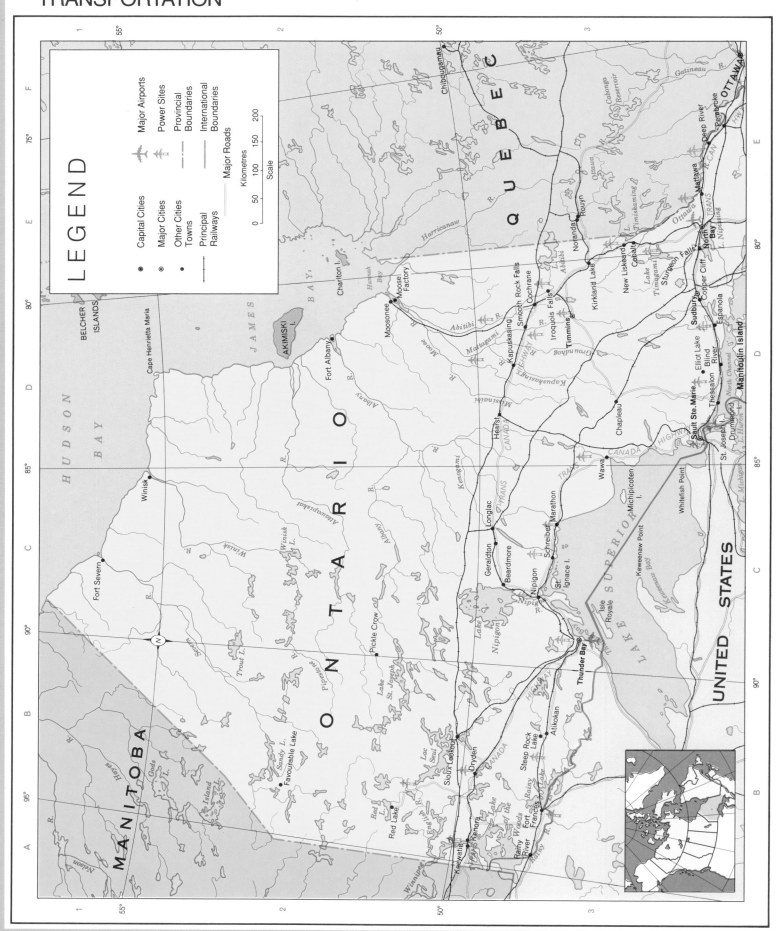

Northern Ontario
LANDFORMS–Relief

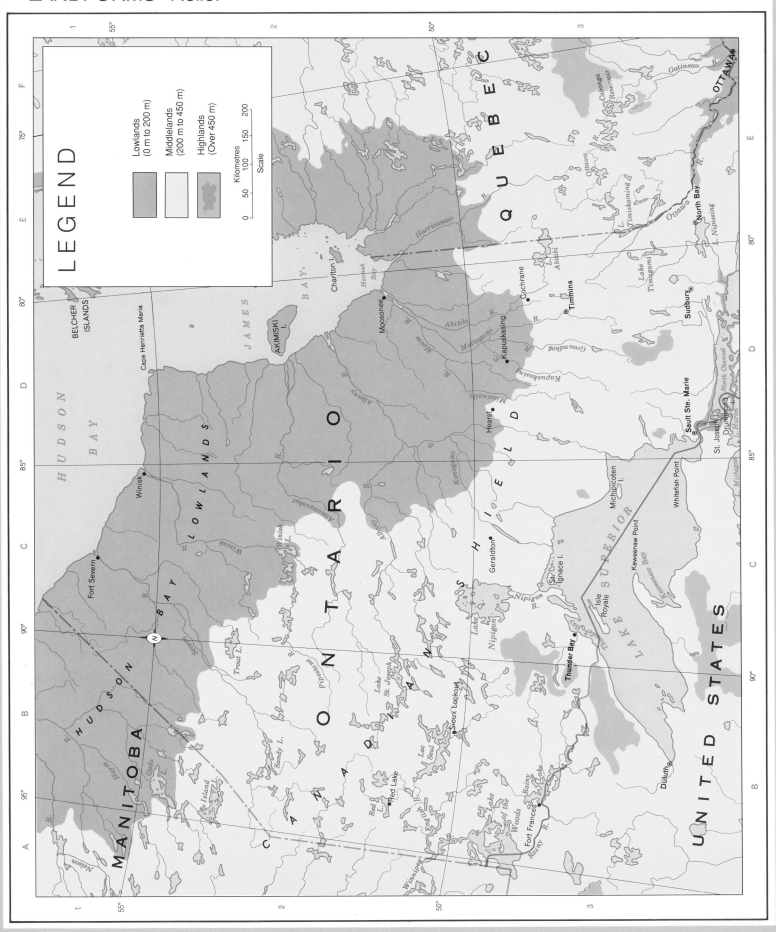

Northern Ontario
MINING and INDUSTRIES

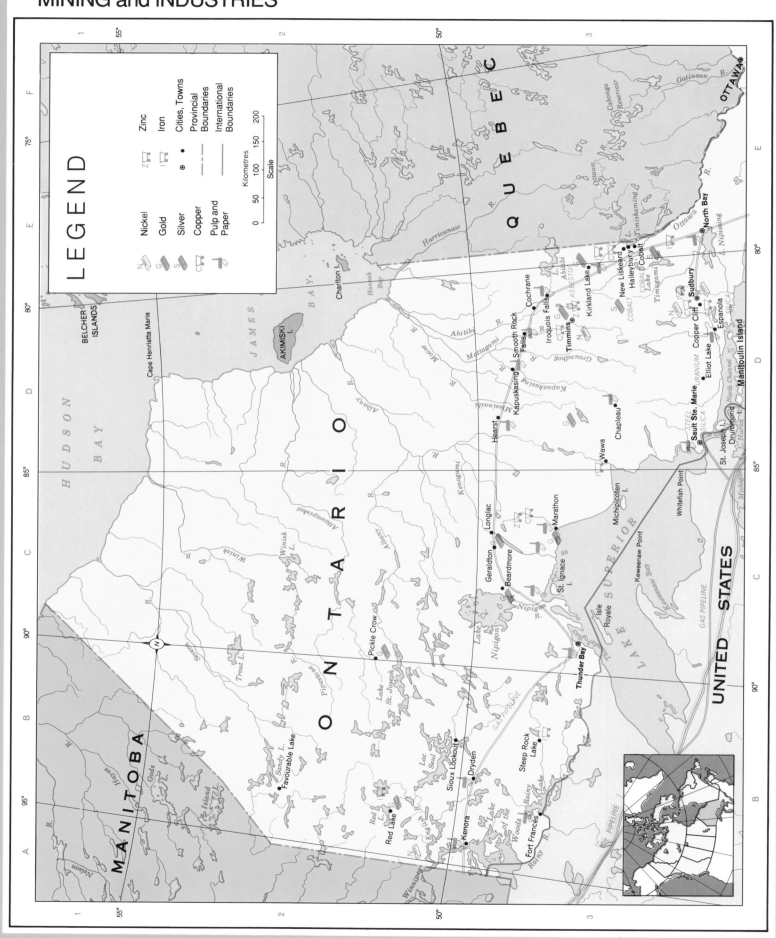

LEGEND

Nickel

Gold

Silver

Copper

Pulp and Paper

Zinc

Iron

Cities, Towns •

Provincial Boundaries

International Boundaries

Scale

Kilometres

0   50   100   150   200

HUDSON BAY

JAMES BAY

BELCHER ISLANDS

AKIMISKI I.

Charlton I.

Hannah Bay

Cape Henrietta Maria

QUEBEC

ONTARIO

MANITOBA

UNITED STATES

OTTAWA

North Bay

Sudbury

Copper Cliff

Espanola

Elliot Lake

Sault Ste. Marie

St. Joseph I.

Drummond I.

Manitoulin Island

New Liskeard

Cobalt

Haileybury

Kirkland Lake

Cochrane

Iroquois Falls

Smooth Rock Falls

Timmins

Kapuskasing

Hearst

Chapleau

Wawa

Michipicoten I.

Whitefish Point

Keweenaw Point

Kaministi Bay

Isle Royale

LAKE SUPERIOR

Marathon

St. Ignace I.

Longlac

Geraldton

Beardmore

Nipigon

Lake Nipigon

Thunder Bay

Pickle Crow

Sioux Lookout

Dryden

Steep Rock Lake

Kenora

Fort Frances

Red Lake

Lake of the Woods

Rainy Lake

Lac Seul

Lake St. Joseph

Trout L.

Sandy L.

Favourable Lake

Island L.

Gods L.

Winnisk L.

Abitibi

Moose R.

Albany R.

Attawapiskat R.

Winisk R.

Severn R.

Nelson R.

Gatineau

Cabonga Reservoir

Timiskaming

Abitibi L.

GAS PIPELINE

OIL PIPELINE

Manitoba
TRANSPORTATION

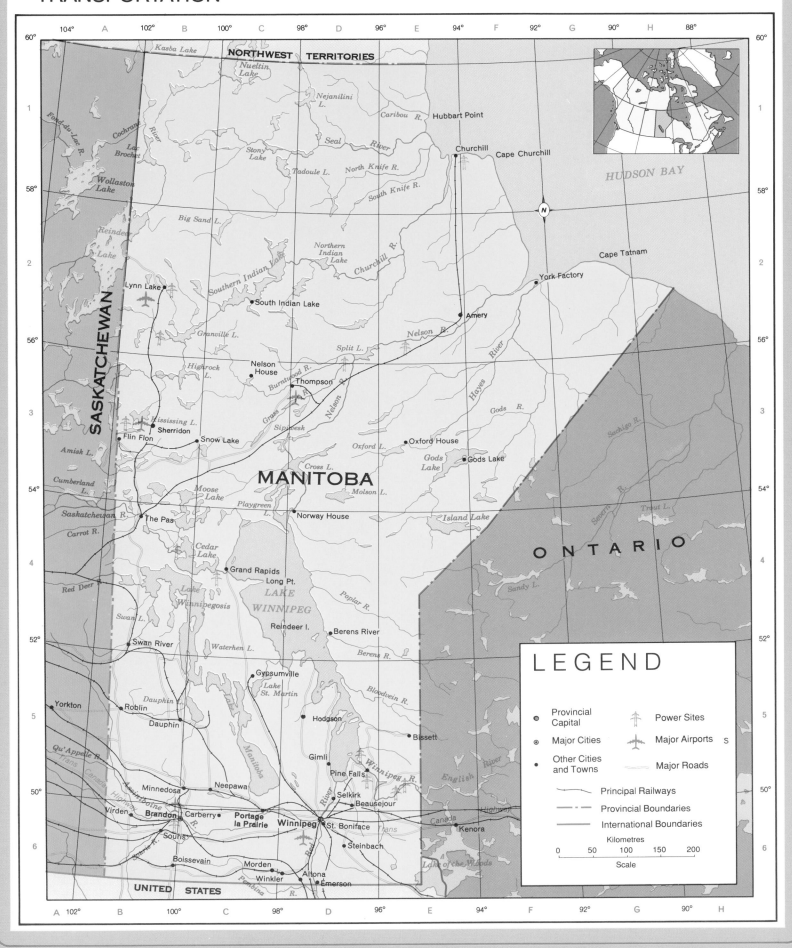

NORTHWEST TERRITORIES

Kasba Lake
Nueltin Lake
Nejanilini L.
Caribou R.
Hubbart Point
Stony Lake
Seal River
Churchill
Cape Churchill
Tadoule L.
North Knife R.
South Knife R.
Big Sand L.
HUDSON BAY
Cape Tatnam
Northern Indian Lake
Churchill R.
Lynn Lake
York Factory
South Indian Lake
Amery
Granville L.
Nelson R.
River
Split L.
Hayes
Highrock L.
Nelson House
Gods R.
Kississing L.
Thompson
Burntwood R.
Sherridon
Grass
Sipiwesk
Nelson
Oxford L.
Oxford House
Sachigo R.
Flin Flon
Snow Lake
Gods Lake
Gods Lake
Amisk L.
MANITOBA
Cross L.
Cumberland L.
Molson L.
Saskatchewan R.
Moose Lake
Playgreen L.
Norway House
Island Lake
Severn R.
Trout L.
The Pas
Carrot R.
ONTARIO
Cedar Lake
Grand Rapids
Long Pt.
Poplar R.
Sandy L.
Red Deer
LAKE WINNIPEGOSIS
LAKE WINNIPEG
Swan L.
Reindeer I.
Berens River
Swan River
Waterhen L.
Berens R.
Bloodvein R.
Yorkton
Gypsumville
Roblin
Dauphin L.
Lake St. Martin
Hodgson
Dauphin
Bissett
English River
Qu'Appelle R.
Gimli
Winnipeg R.
Minnedosa
Neepawa
Pine Falls
Virden
Brandon
Carberry
Portage la Prairie
Selkirk
Winnipeg
Beausejour
Kenora
Souris
St. Boniface
Canada
Boissevain
Steinbach
Morden
Altona
Winkler
Emerson
UNITED STATES
Pembina R.
Lake of the Woods
Cochrane
Fond-du-Lac R.
Lac Brochet
Wollaston Lake
Reindeer Lake
Southern Indian Lake
SASKATCHEWAN

LEGEND

- ● Provincial Capital
- ◎ Major Cities
- • Other Cities and Towns
- ⟰ Power Sites
- ✈ Major Airports
- ～ Major Roads
- — Principal Railways
- —·— Provincial Boundaries
- — International Boundaries

Kilometres
0 50 100 150 200
Scale

Manitoba
LANDFORMS–Relief

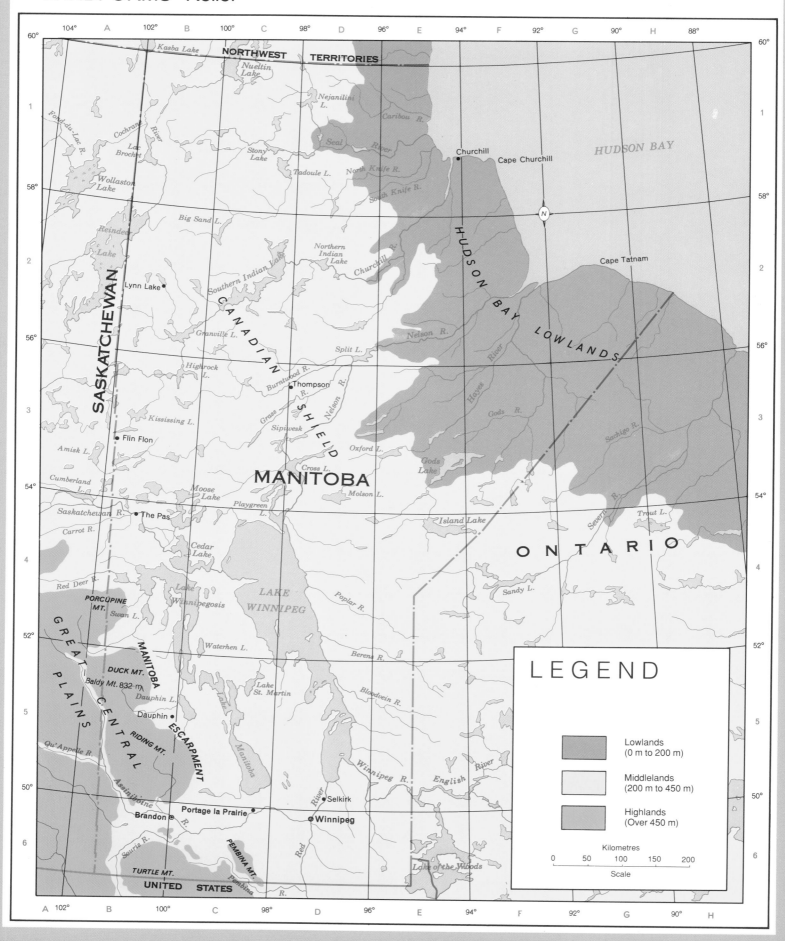

NORTHWEST TERRITORIES

Kasba Lake

Nueltin Lake

Nejanilini L.

Fond-du-Lac R.

Cochrane River

Caribou R.

HUDSON BAY

Seal *River*

Churchill

Cape Churchill

Lac Brochet

Stony Lake

Tadoule L.

North Knife R.

N

Wollaston Lake

Big Sand L.

South Knife R.

SASKATCHEWAN

Reindeer Lake

H U D S O N   B A Y

Cape Tatnam

Lynn Lake

Southern Indian Lake

Northern Indian Lake

Churchill R.

Nelson R.

L O W L A N D S

C A N A D I A N

Granville L.

Split L.

Highrock L.

Burntwood R.

Thompson

Nelson R.

Hayes

River

Gods R.

Sachigo R.

Flin Flon

Kississing L.

Grass R.

Sipiwesk L.

S H I E L D

Amisk L.

Oxford L.

MANITOBA

Gods Lake

Cumberland L.

Cross L.

Moose Lake

Molson L.

Saskatchewan R.

The Pas

Playgreen L.

Island Lake

Severn R.

Trout L.

Carrot R.

Cedar Lake

O N T A R I O

Red Deer R.

Lake Winnipegosis

L A K E   W I N N I P E G

Poplar R.

Sandy L.

PORCUPINE MT.

Swan L.

G R E A T

MANITOBA

Berens R.

Waterhen L.

DUCK MT.

Baldy Mt. 832 m

Dauphin L.

Lake St. Martin

Bloodvein R.

P L A I N S

Dauphin

RIDING MT.

ESCARPMENT

Lake Manitoba

C E N T R A L

Qu'Appelle R.

Assiniboine R.

Winnipeg R.

English *River*

Brandon

Portage la Prairie

Red River

Selkirk

Winnipeg

Souris R.

PEMBINA MT.

Assiniboine R.

Red R.

Lake of the Woods

TURTLE MT.

Pembina R.

UNITED STATES

LEGEND

Lowlands
(0 m to 200 m)

Middlelands
(200 m to 450 m)

Highlands
(Over 450 m)

Kilometres

0   50   100   150   200

Scale

Manitoba
FARMING

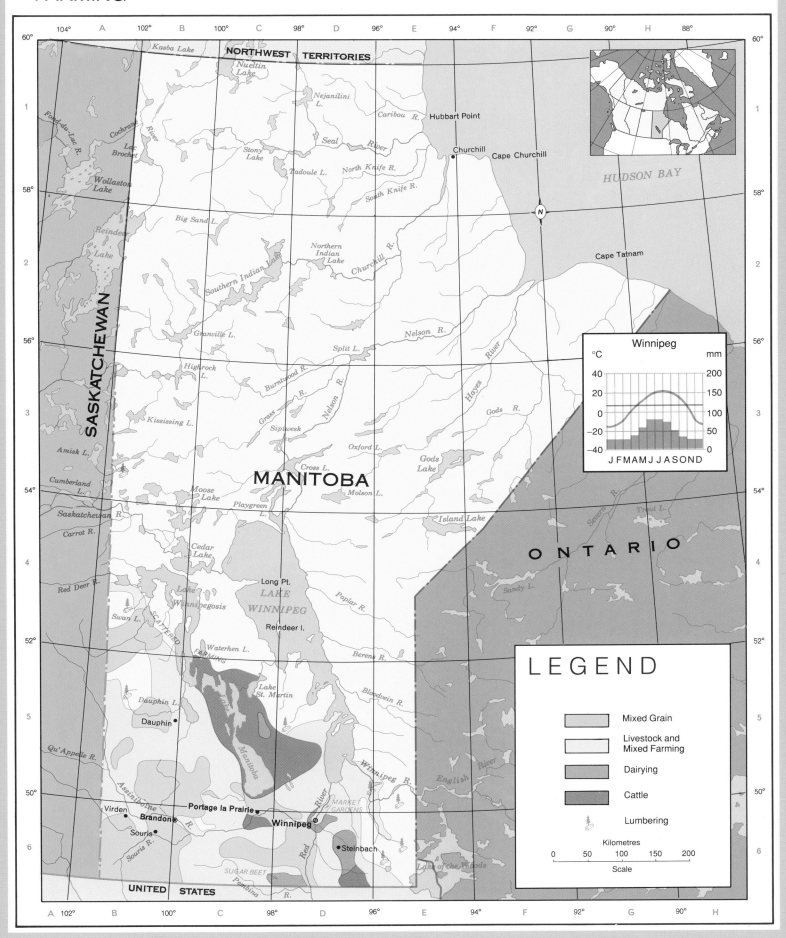

LEGEND

	Mixed Grain
	Livestock and Mixed Farming
	Dairying
	Cattle
	Lumbering

Kilometres

0   50   100   150   200

Scale

Winnipeg

°C / mm

J F M A M J J A S O N D

SASKATCHEWAN

NORTHWEST TERRITORIES

Kasba Lake
Nueltin Lake
Nejanilini L.
Caribou R.
Hubbart Point
Seal River
Churchill
Cape Churchill
HUDSON BAY
Stony Lake
Tadoule L.
North Knife R.
South Knife R.
Cape Tatnam
Fond-du-Lac R.
Cochrane River
Lac Brochet
Wollaston Lake
Reindeer Lake
Big Sand L.
Northern Indian Lake
Churchill R.
Nelson R.
Southern Indian Lake
Granville L.
Split L.
Nelson River
Amisk L.
Highrock L.
Burntwood R.
Grass R.
Nelson R.
Hayes River
Gods R.
Kississing L.
Sipiwesk L.
Oxford L.
Cumberland L.
Saskatchewan R.
Carrot R.
Moose Lake
Cross L.
MANITOBA
Molson L.
Gods Lake
Playgreen L.
Island Lake
Cedar Lake
Red Deer R.
Lake Winnipegosis
LAKE WINNIPEG
Poplar R.
Sandy L.
ONTARIO
Trout L.
Severn River
Swan L.
SCATTERED FARMING
Waterhen L.
Reindeer I.
Berens R.
Long Pt.
Lake St. Martin
Bloodvein R.
Dauphin L.
Dauphin
Lake Manitoba
Winnipeg R.
English River
Qu'Appelle R.
Assiniboine R.
Virden
Brandon
Portage la Prairie
MARKET GARDENS
Winnipeg
Red River
Souris
Souris R.
Steinbach
Lake of the Woods
SUGAR BEET
Pembina R.
UNITED STATES

Manitoba
MINING and INDUSTRIES

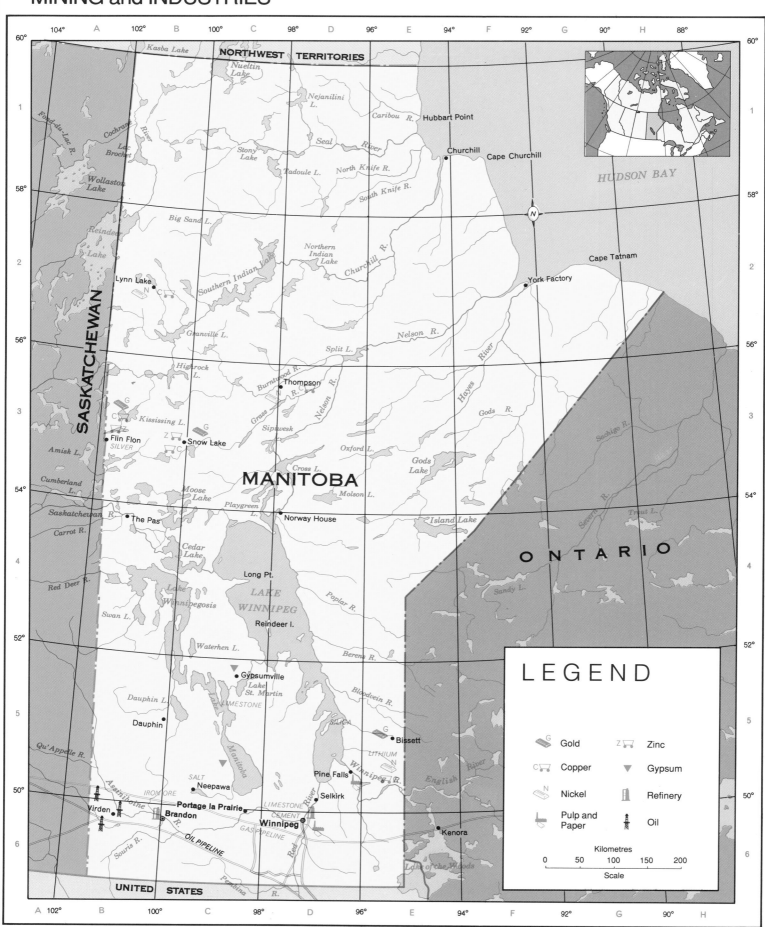

NORTHWEST TERRITORIES

Kasba Lake

Nueltin Lake

Fond-du-Lac R.

Cochrane

Lac Brochet

River

Nejanilini L.

Caribou R.

Hubbart Point

Churchill

Cape Churchill

HUDSON BAY

Wollaston Lake

Reindeer Lake

Stony Lake

Seal River

North Knife R.

Tadoule L.

South Knife R.

Cape Tatnam

SASKATCHEWAN

Big Sand L.

Southern Indian Lake

Northern Indian Lake

Churchill R.

York Factory

Lynn Lake

Granville L.

Nelson R.

River

Amisk L.

Highrock L.

Kississing L.

Burntwood R.

Thompson

Grass R.

Split L.

Nelson R.

Hayes River

Gods R.

Flin Flon
SILVER

Snow Lake

Sipiwesk

Oxford L.

Gods Lake

Sachigo R.

Cumberland L.

MANITOBA

Cross L.

Gods Lake

Saskatchewan R.

The Pas

Moose Lake

Playgreen L.

Norway House

Molson L.

Island Lake

Severn R.

Trout L.

Carrot R.

Red Deer R.

Cedar Lake

ONTARIO

Lake Winnipegosis

Long Pt.

LAKE WINNIPEG

Poplar R.

Sandy L.

Swan L.

Reindeer I.

Waterhen L.

Berens R.

Bloodvein R.

Gypsumville
Lake St. Martin

Qu'Appelle R.

Dauphin L.

LIMESTONE

SILICA

Bissett

Dauphin

Manitoba

English River

Kenora

LITHIUM

Virden

Assiniboine R.

SALT

IRON ORE

Neepawa

Portage la Prairie

Brandon

Pine Falls

Selkirk

LIMESTONE

Winnipeg R.

Winnipeg

CEMENT

OIL PIPELINE

GAS PIPELINE

Red River

Souris R.

Pembina R.

Lake of the Woods

UNITED STATES

LEGEND

Gold		Zinc	
Copper		Gypsum	
Nickel		Refinery	
Pulp and Paper		Oil	

Kilometres

0   50   100   150   200

Scale

Saskatchewan
TRANSPORTATION

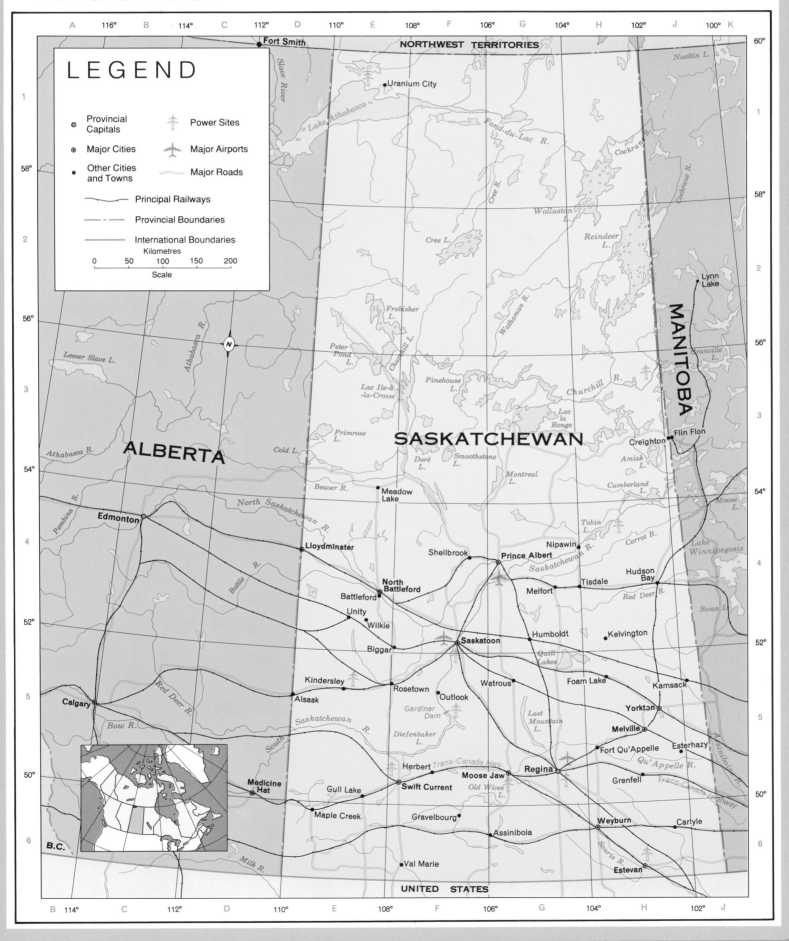

LEGEND

- ◉ Provincial Capitals
- ◎ Major Cities
- ● Other Cities and Towns
- ⌁ Power Sites
- ✈ Major Airports
- ∿ Major Roads

Principal Railways
Provincial Boundaries
International Boundaries

Kilometres
0 50 100 150 200
Scale

ALBERTA

SASKATCHEWAN

MANITOBA

NORTHWEST TERRITORIES

UNITED STATES

B.C.

Fort Smith
Uranium City
Nueltin L.
Lynn Lake
Flin Flon
Creighton
Lesser Slave L.
Lac Île-à-la-Crosse
Primrose L.
Cold L.
Meadow Lake
Edmonton
Lloydminster
Shellbrook
Nipawin
Prince Albert
North Battleford
Battleford
Melfort
Tisdale
Hudson Bay
Unity
Wilkie
Humboldt
Kelvington
Biggar
Saskatoon
Kindersley
Rosetown
Watrous
Foam Lake
Kamsack
Alsask
Outlook
Calgary
Yorkton
Melville
Esterhazy
Fort Qu'Appelle
Herbert
Moose Jaw
Regina
Grenfell
Medicine Hat
Gull Lake
Swift Current
Maple Creek
Gravelbourg
Weyburn
Carlyle
Assiniboia
Val Marie
Estevan

Saskatchewan
LANDFORMS–Relief

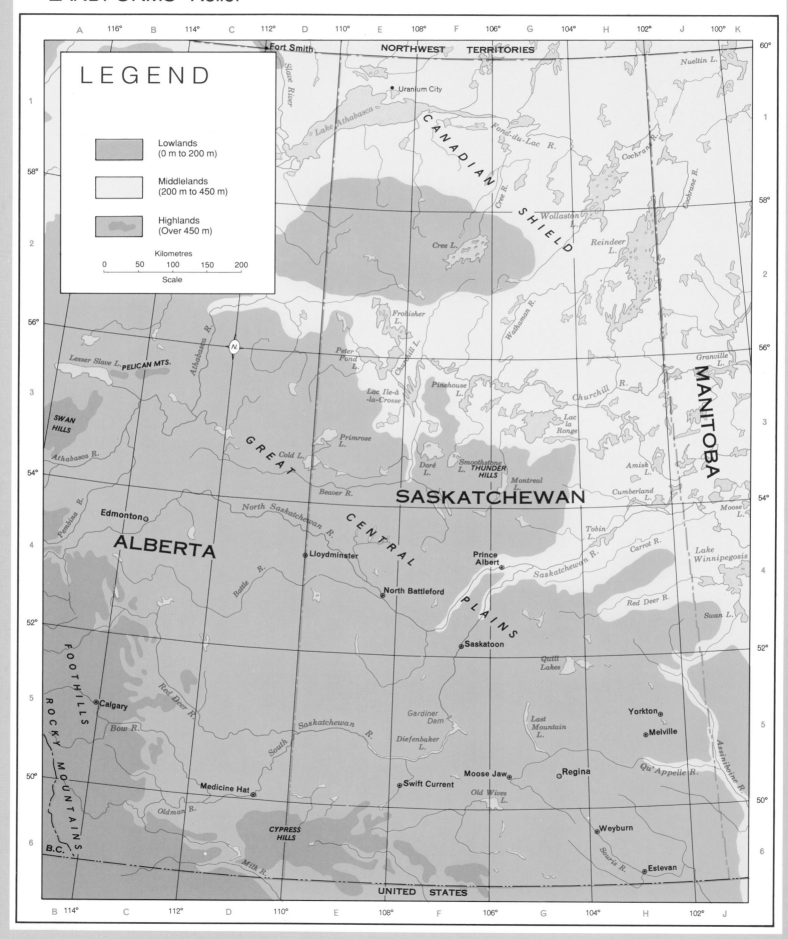

LEGEND

Lowlands
(0 m to 200 m)

Middlelands
(200 m to 450 m)

Highlands
(Over 450 m)

Kilometres

0   50   100   150   200

Scale

Saskatchewan
FARMING

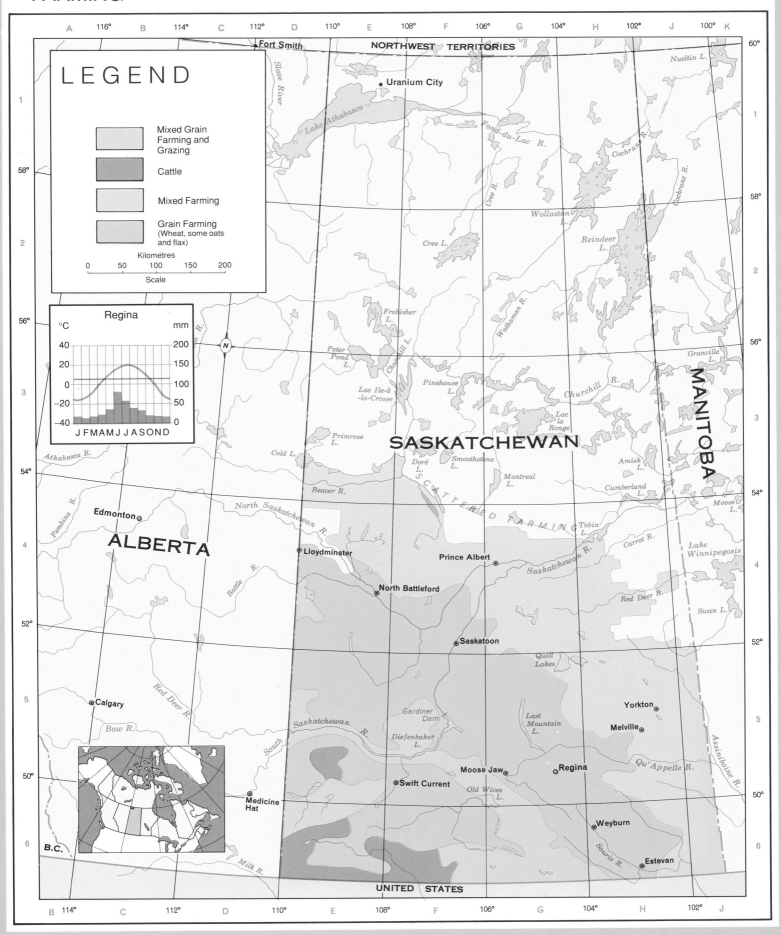

LEGEND

Mixed Grain Farming and Grazing

Cattle

Mixed Farming

Grain Farming (Wheat, some oats and flax)

Kilométres

0 50 100 150 200

Scale

Regina

°C — mm

40 — 200
20 — 150
0 — 100
-20 — 50
-40 — 0

J F M A M J J A S O N D

NORTHWEST TERRITORIES

Fort Smith

Uranium City

Lake Athabasca

Nueltin L.

Slave River

Fond-du-Lac R.

Cochrane R.

Cree R.

Wollaston L.

Cree L.

Reindeer L.

Wathaman R.

Frobisher L.

Churchill L.

Granville L.

Peter Pond L.

Pinehouse L.

Churchill R.

MANITOBA

Lac Ile-à-la-Crosse

Lac la Ronge

Amisk L.

Primrose L.

SASKATCHEWAN

Doré L.

Smoothstone L.

Cold L.

Montreal L.

Cumberland L.

Moose L.

Athabasca R.

Beaver R.

SCATTERED FARMING

Pembina R.

North Saskatchewan R.

Tobin L.

Carrot R.

Lake Winnipegosis

Edmonton

ALBERTA

Lloydminster

Prince Albert

Saskatchewan R.

Red Deer R.

Swan L.

Battle R.

North Battleford

Saskatoon

Quill Lakes

Calgary

Red Deer R.

Gardiner Dam

Last Mountain L.

Yorkton

Melville

Bow R.

South Saskatchewan R.

Diefenbaker L.

Moose Jaw

Regina

Qu'Appelle R.

Assiniboine R.

Swift Current

Old Wives L.

Medicine Hat

Weyburn

B.C.

Milk R.

Souris R.

Estevan

UNITED STATES

Saskatchewan
MINING and INDUSTRIES

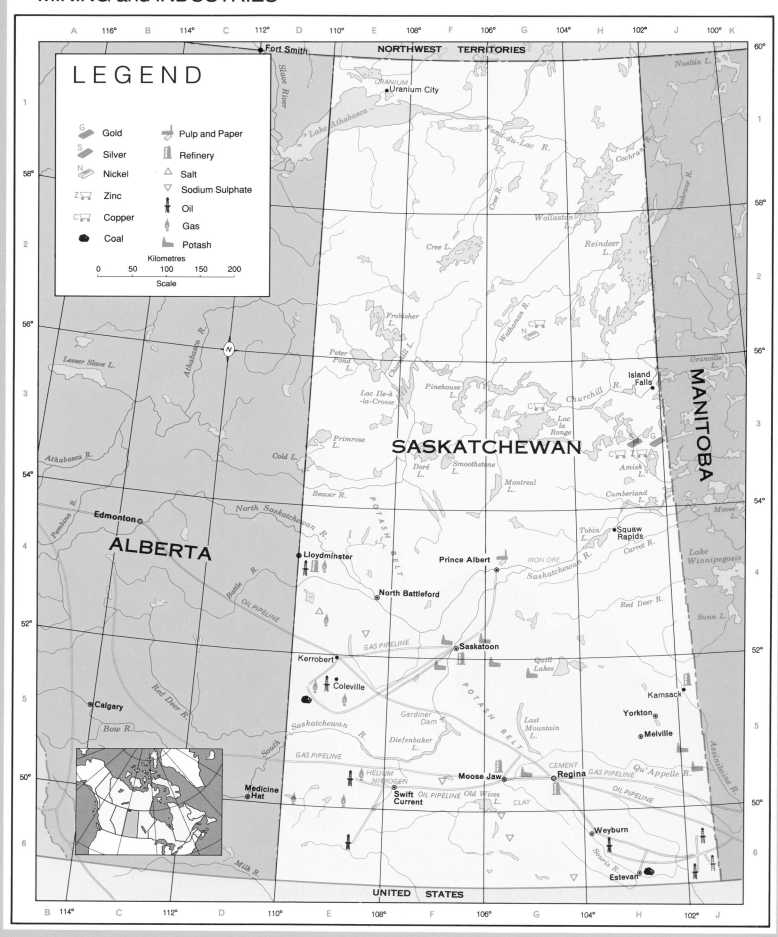

LEGEND

G	Gold		Pulp and Paper
S	Silver		Refinery
N	Nickel	△	Salt
Z	Zinc	▽	Sodium Sulphate
C	Copper		Oil
	Coal		Gas
			Potash

Kilometres

0 50 100 150 200

Scale

Alberta
TRANSPORTATION

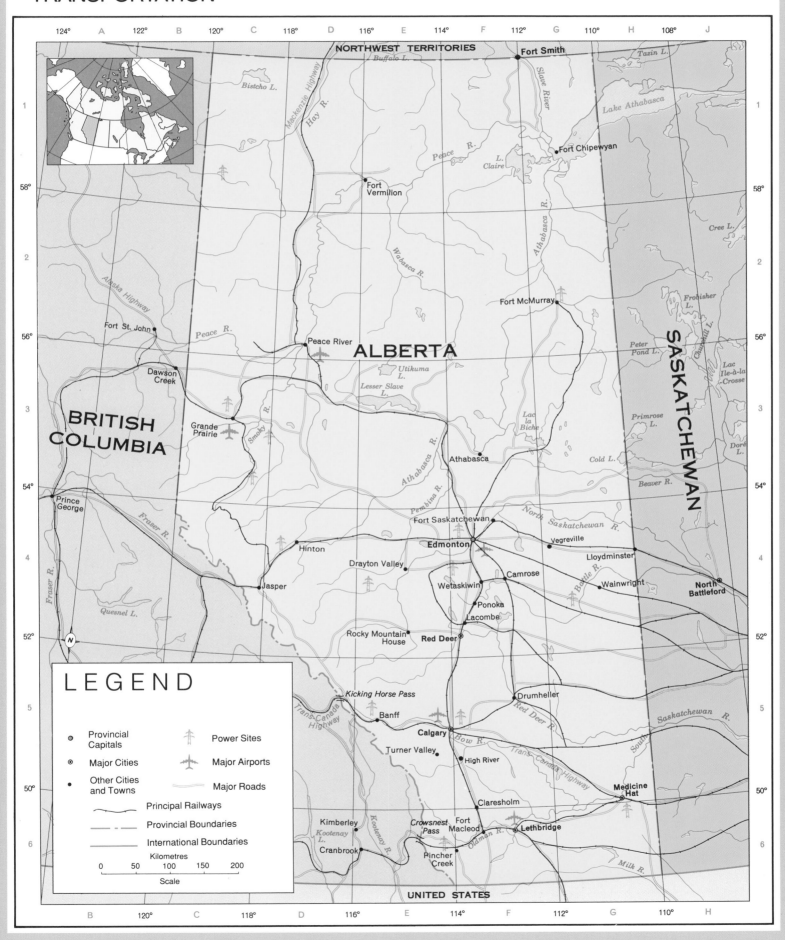

124° A 122° B 120° C 118° D 116° E 114° F 112° G 110° H 108° J

NORTHWEST TERRITORIES

Fort Smith

Buffalo L.

Bistcho L.

Tazin L.

Slave River

Lake Athabasca

Mackenzie Highway

Hay R.

Peace R.

L. Claire

•Fort Chipewyan

58°

Fort Vermilion

Cree L.

Wabasca R.

2

Athabasca R.

Frobisher L.

Alaska Highway

Fort McMurray

SASKATCHEWAN

56°

Fort St. John

Peace R.

Peace River ALBERTA

Utikuma L.

Peter Pond L.

Churchill L.

Lac Ile-à-la-Crosse

Dawson Creek

Lesser Slave L.

3

BRITISH COLUMBIA

Grande Prairie

Smoky R.

Lac la Biche

Primrose L.

Doré L.

Athabasca

Cold L.

54°

Prince George

Fraser R.

Athabasca R.

Beaver R.

North Saskatchewan R.

Fort Saskatchewan

Vegreville

Fraser R.

Pembina R.

Edmonton

Lloydminster

Hinton

Drayton Valley

Camrose

Battle R.

Wainwright

North Battleford

Wetaskiwin

Jasper

Ponoka
Lacombe

Quesnel L.

Rocky Mountain House

Red Deer

52°

N

LEGEND

Kicking Horse Pass

Drumheller

Red Deer R.

5

Trans-Canada Highway

Banff

Saskatchewan R.

• Provincial Capitals

⚜ Power Sites

Calgary

Bow R.

Trans-Canada Highway

◉ Major Cities

✈ Major Airports

Turner Valley

High River

• Other Cities and Towns

Major Roads

50°

Medicine Hat

Principal Railways

Claresholm

South Saskatchewan R.

Provincial Boundaries

Kimberley

Crowsnest Pass

Fort Macleod

◉Lethbridge

International Boundaries

Kootenay L.

Kootenay R.

Oldman R.

Kilometres

0 50 100 150 200

Cranbrook

Pincher Creek

Milk R.

Scale

6

UNITED STATES

B 120° C 118° D 116° E 114° F 112° G 110° H

Alberta
LANDFORMS—Relief

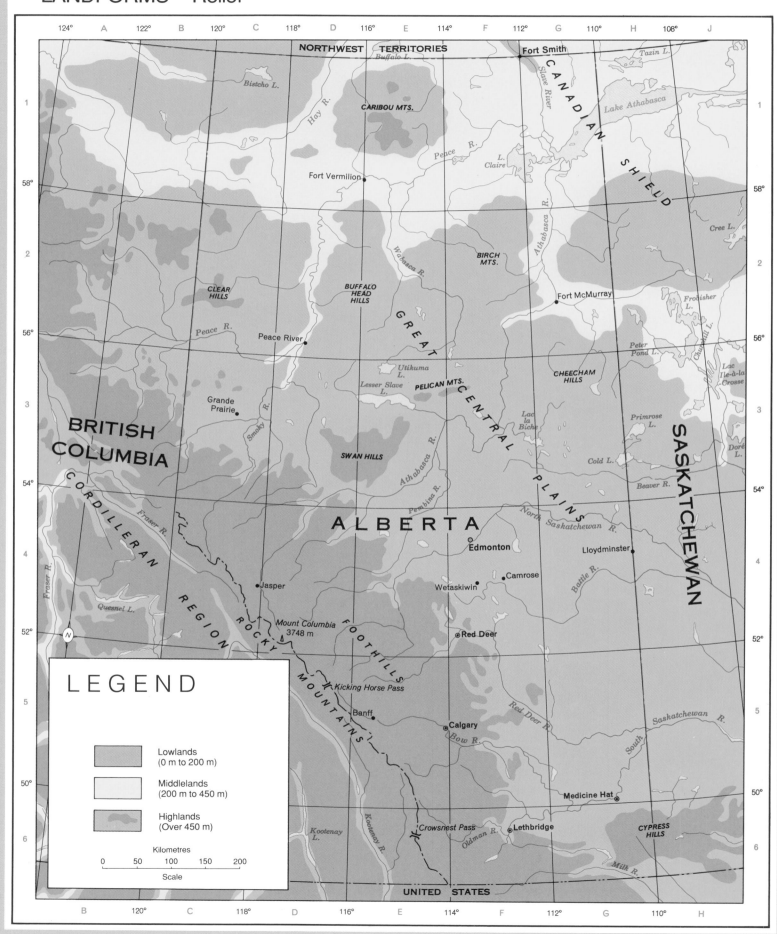

NORTHWEST TERRITORIES

Fort Smith

BRITISH COLUMBIA

Buffalo L.

Bistcho L.

CARIBOU MTS.

Hay R.

Fort Vermilion

CLEAR HILLS

BUFFALO HEAD HILLS

Wabasca R.

BIRCH MTS.

GREAT

Peace R.

L. Claire

CANADIAN SHIELD

Lake Athabasca

Cree L.

Fort McMurray

Frobisher L.

Athabasca R.

CENTRAL

Peace River

Peace R.

Utikuma L.

Lesser Slave L.

PELICAN MTS.

CHEECHAM HILLS

Peter Pond L.

Primrose L.

Lac Ile-à-la-Crosse

Doré L.

SASKATCHEWAN

Grande Prairie

Smoky R.

SWAN HILLS

Lac la Biche

Athabasca R.

PLAINS

Cold L.

CORDILLERAN REGION

Fraser R.

Pembina R.

ALBERTA

North Saskatchewan R.

Edmonton

Battle R.

Lloydminster

Quesnel L.

Jasper

FOOTHILLS

Wetaskiwin

Camrose

Beaver R.

Mount Columbia 3748 m

ROCKY

Red Deer

MOUNTAINS

Kicking Horse Pass

Banff

Calgary

Bow R.

Red Deer R.

Saskatchewan R.

South Saskatchewan R.

Fraser R.

Medicine Hat

Kootenay L.

Kootenay R.

Crowsnest Pass

Lethbridge

CYPRESS HILLS

Oldman R.

Milk R.

UNITED STATES

LEGEND

	Lowlands (0 m to 200 m)
	Middlelands (200 m to 450 m)
	Highlands (Over 450 m)

Kilometres

0   50   100   150   200

Scale

Alberta
FARMING

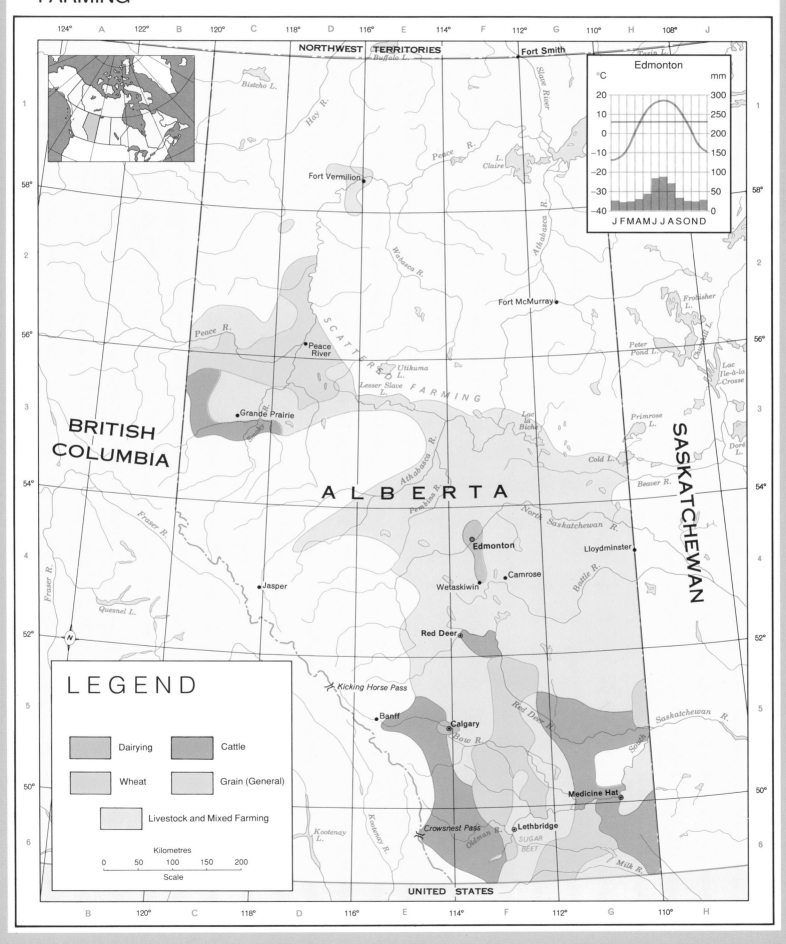

LEGEND

- Dairying
- Cattle
- Wheat
- Grain (General)
- Livestock and Mixed Farming

Kilometres
0   50   100   150   200
Scale

Edmonton
°C   mm
20   300
10   250
0   200
-10   150
-20   100
-30   50
-40   0
J F M A M J J A S O N D

Alberta
MINING and INDUSTRIES

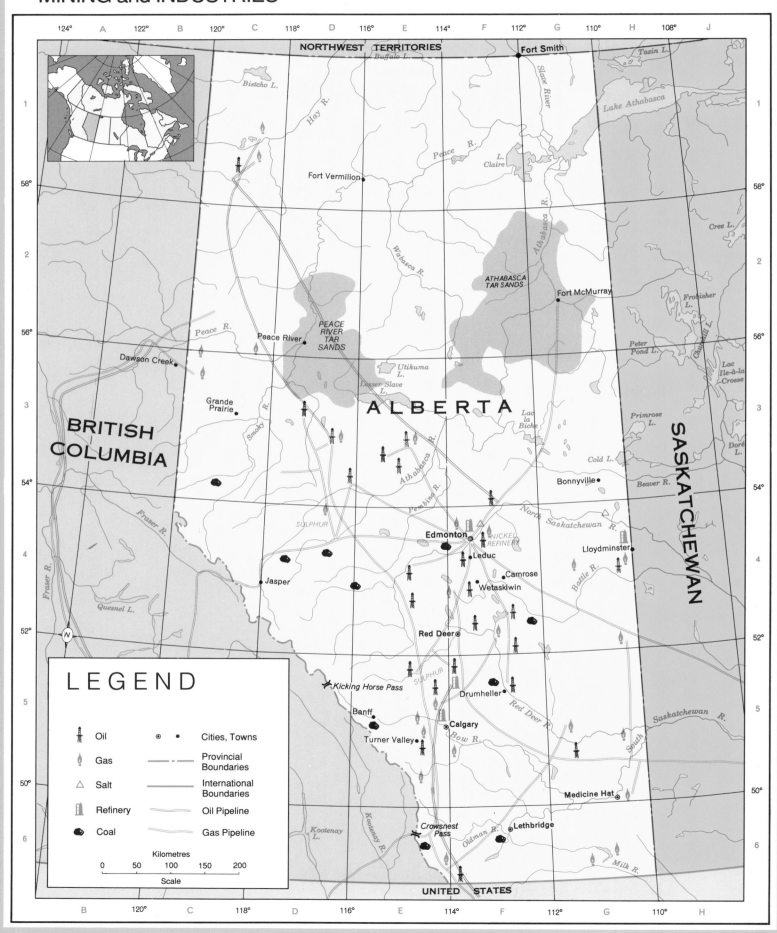

NORTHWEST TERRITORIES

Fort Smith

Buffalo L.

Bistcho L.

Hay R.

Tazin L.

Slave River

Lake Athabasca

Fort Vermilion

Peace R.

L. Claire

Cree L.

Athabasca R.

Wabasca R.

ATHABASCA TAR SANDS

Fort McMurray

Frobisher L.

BRITISH COLUMBIA

Peace R.

Peace River

PEACE RIVER TAR SANDS

Utikuma L.

Lesser Slave L.

ALBERTA

Peter Pond L.

Lac Ile-à-la-Crosse

Dawson Creek

Grande Prairie

Smoky R.

Lac la Biche

Primrose L.

SASKATCHEWAN

Cold L.

Doré L.

Bonnyville

Beaver R.

Athabasca R.

Pembina R.

SULPHUR

North Saskatchewan R.

Edmonton

NICKEL REFINERY

Lloydminster

Battle R.

Jasper

Leduc

Camrose

Wetaskiwin

Quesnel L.

Red Deer

Fraser R.

Red Deer R.

SULPHUR

Drumheller

Saskatchewan R.

Kicking Horse Pass

Banff

Calgary

Bow R.

Turner Valley

South Saskatchewan R.

LEGEND

Oil		Cities, Towns	
Gas		Provincial Boundaries	
Salt		International Boundaries	
Refinery		Oil Pipeline	
Coal		Gas Pipeline	

Kilometres

0   50   100   150   200

Scale

Medicine Hat

Kootenay L.

Kootenay R.

Crowsnest Pass

Oldman R.

Lethbridge

Milk R.

UNITED STATES

British Columbia
TRANSPORTATION

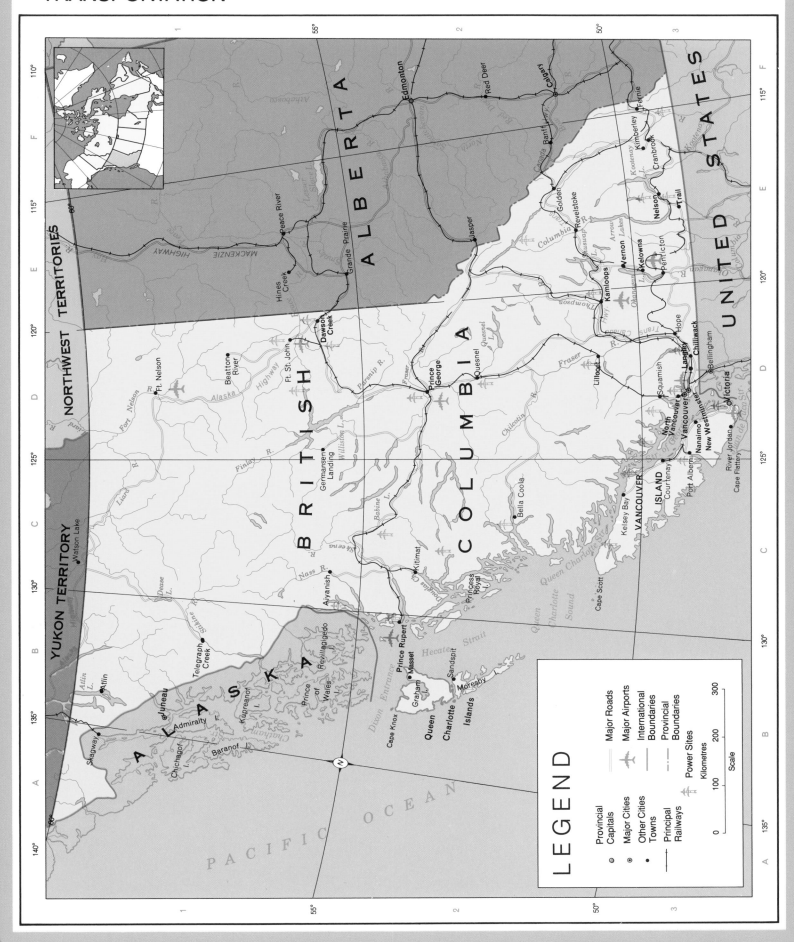

LEGEND

Provincial Capitals ⊙
Major Cities ⊚
Other Cities Towns •
Principal Railways
Power Sites ✈
Major Roads
Major Airports ✈
International Boundaries
Provincial Boundaries

Scale
Kilometres
0 100 200 300

British Columbia
LANDFORMS—Relief

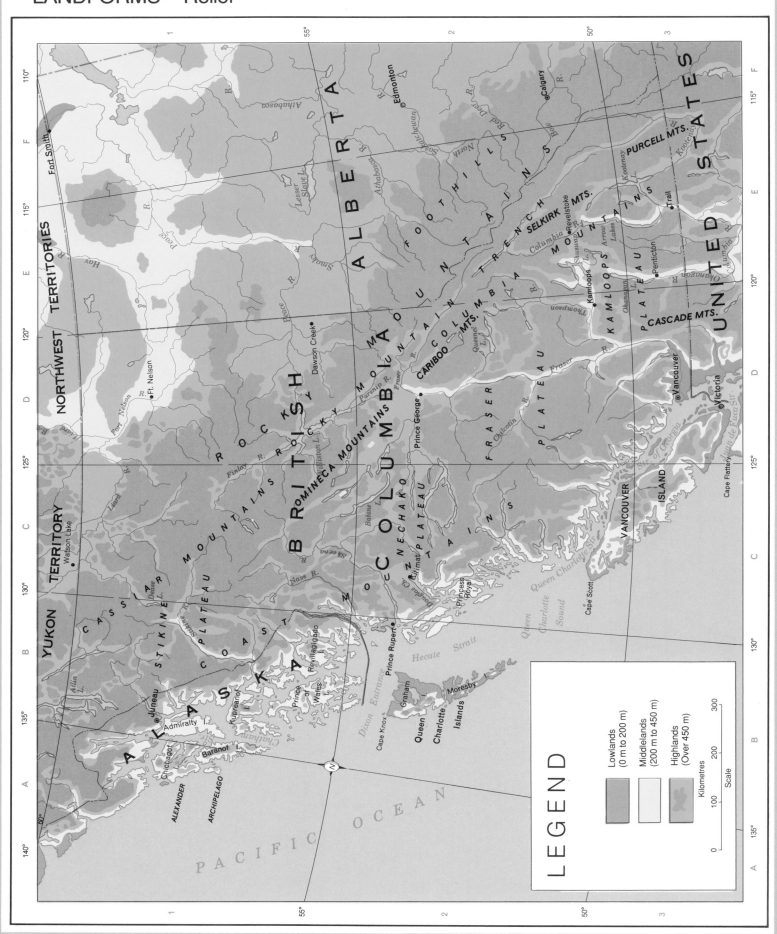

LEGEND

Lowlands (0 m to 200 m)

Middlelands (200 m to 450 m)

Highlands (Over 450 m)

Kilometres

0 100 200 300

Scale

British Columbia
FARMING

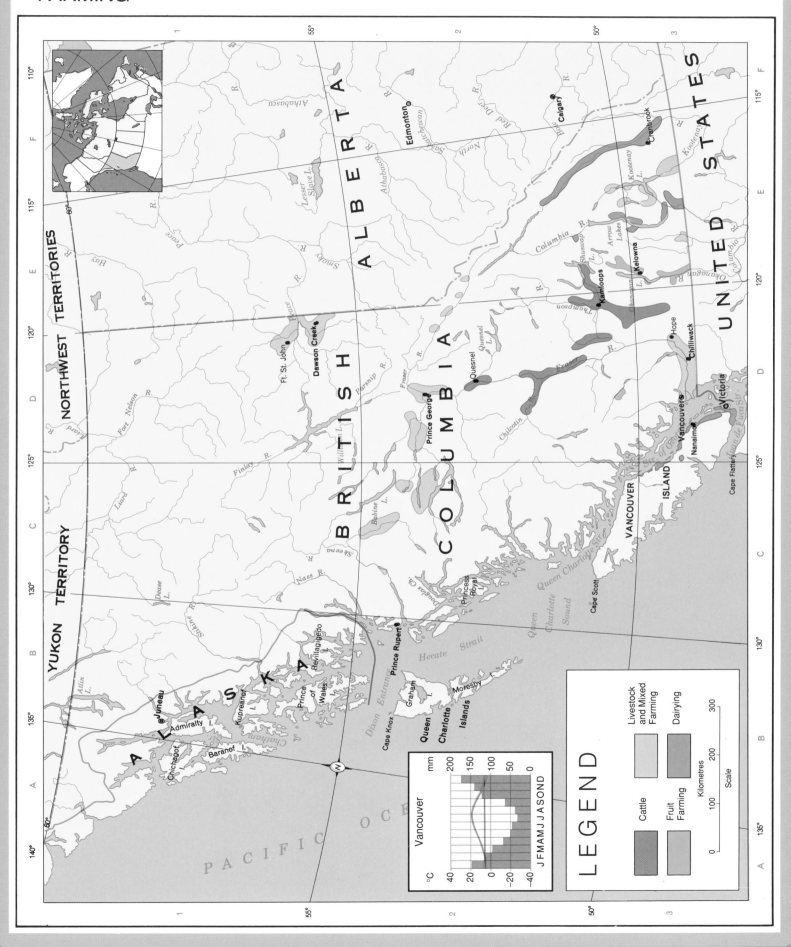

LEGEND

Cattle

Fruit Farming

Livestock and Mixed Farming

Dairying

Scale
Kilometres
0   100   200   300

Vancouver

mm
200
150
100
50
0

°C
40
20
0
-20
-40

J F M A M J J A S O N D

PACIFIC OCEAN

ALASKA

YUKON TERRITORY

NORTHWEST TERRITORIES

BRITISH COLUMBIA

ALBERTA

UNITED STATES

Edmonton

Calgary

Cranbrook

Kamloops

Kelowna

Hope

Chilliwack

Quesnel

Prince George

Victoria

Vancouver

Nanaimo

Dawson Creek

Ft. St. John

Prince Rupert

Juneau

VANCOUVER ISLAND

Queen Charlotte Islands

Graham I.

Moresby I.

Baranof I.

Chichagof I.

Admiralty I.

Kupreanof I.

Prince of Wales I.

Revillagigedo I.

Princess Royal I.

Athabasca R.

Peace R.

Hay R.

Smoky R.

Lesser Slave L.

Liard R.

Deese L.

Atlin L.

Finlay R.

Parsnip R.

Fraser R.

Nass R.

Skeena R.

Babine L.

Stikine R.

Williston L.

Chilcotin R.

Thompson R.

Columbia R.

Shuswap L.

Arrow Lakes

Kootenay L.

Okanagan L.

North Saskatchewan R.

Red Deer R.

Bow R.

Fort Nelson R.

Dixon Entrance

Hecate Strait

Queen Charlotte Sound

Queen Charlotte Strait

Strait of Georgia

Juan de Fuca Str.

Cape Flattery

Cape Scott

Cape Knox

Douglas Chan.

N

60°

55°

50°

140°   135°   130°   125°   120°   115°   110°

A B C D E F

British Columbia
MINING and INDUSTRIES

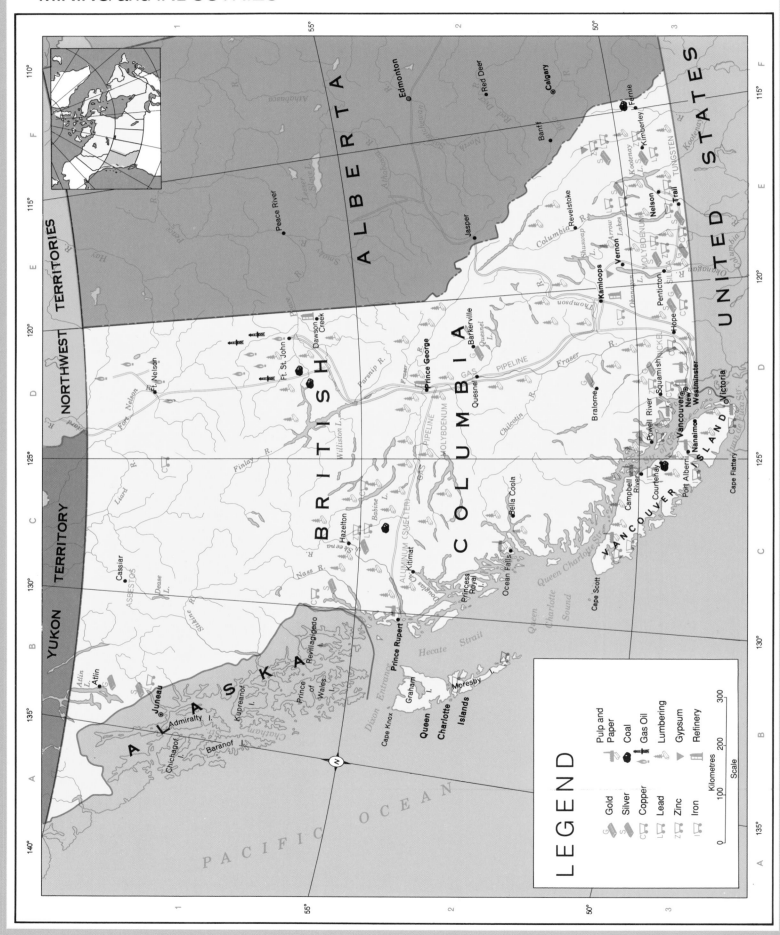

LEGEND

G.	Gold		Pulp and Paper
S.	Silver		Coal
	Copper		Gas Oil
	Lead		Lumbering
Z.	Zinc		Gypsum
	Iron		Refinery

Scale
Kilometres
0   100   200   300

The St. Lawrence Seaway System

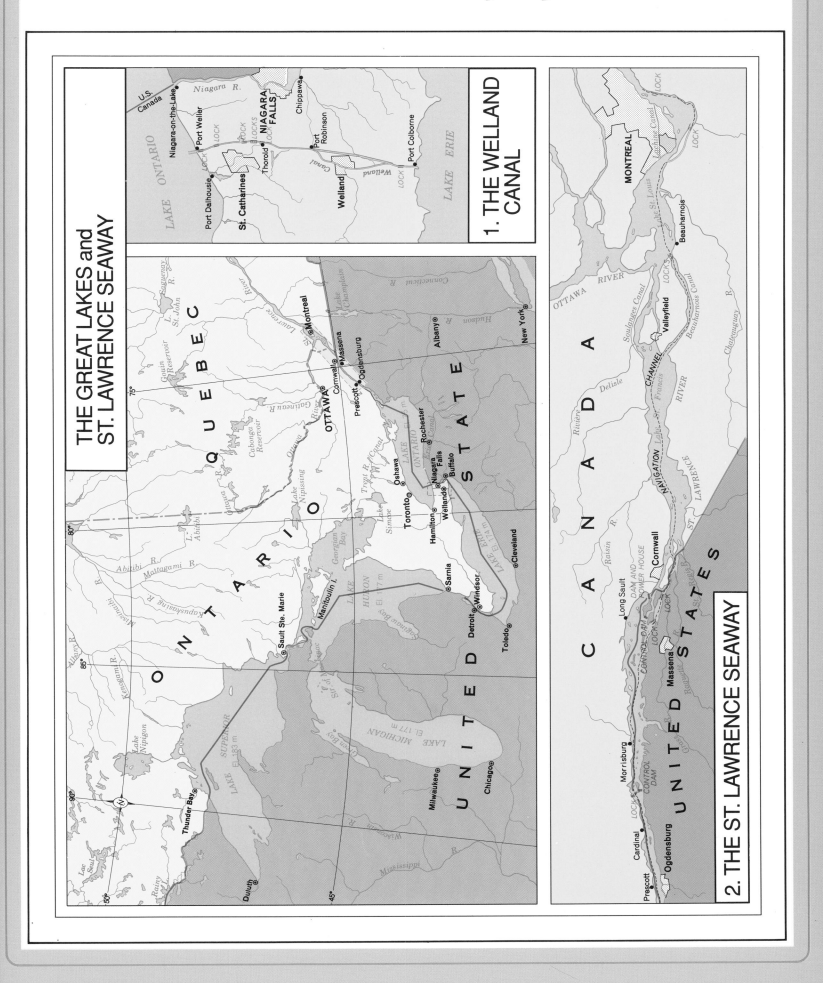

Canada
THE NORTHLAND

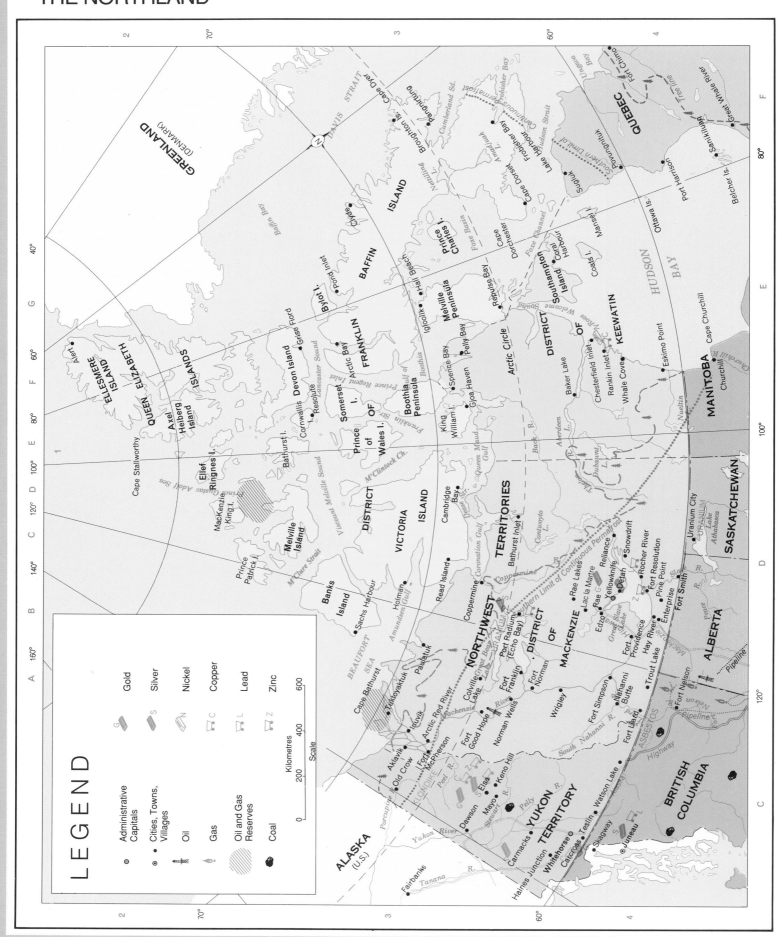

Holman Island, NWT

Whitehorse, YT

Yellowknife, NWT

Whitehorse

°C mm
20 — 150
10 — 125
0 — 100
-10 — 75
-20 — 50
-30 — 25
-40 — 0
J F M A M J J A S O N D

Yellowknife

°C mm
150
30 — 125
20 — 100
10 — 75
0 — 50
-10 — 25
-20 — 0
-30
J F M A M J J A S O N D

The United States
POLITICAL DIVISIONS—(excluding Alaska and Hawaii)

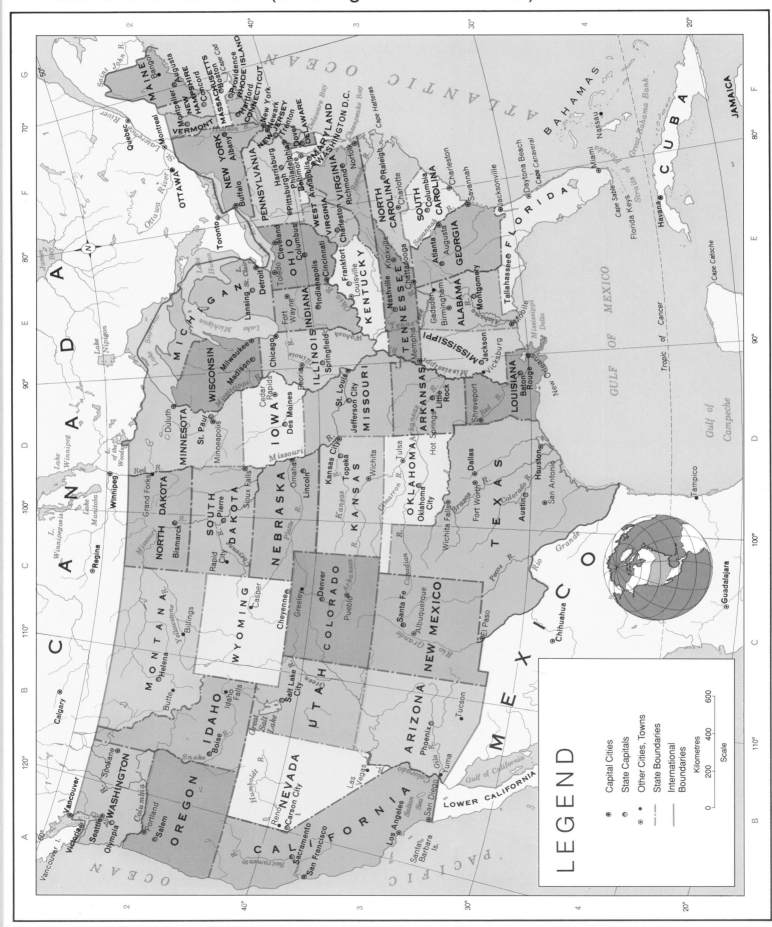

LEGEND

- ◉ Capital Cities
- ◎ State Capitals
- ◉ Other Cities, Towns
- --- State Boundaries
- — International Boundaries

Kilometres
0   200   400   600

Scale

Houston, TX

San Francisco, CA

New York, NY

The United States
LANDFORMS—Relief

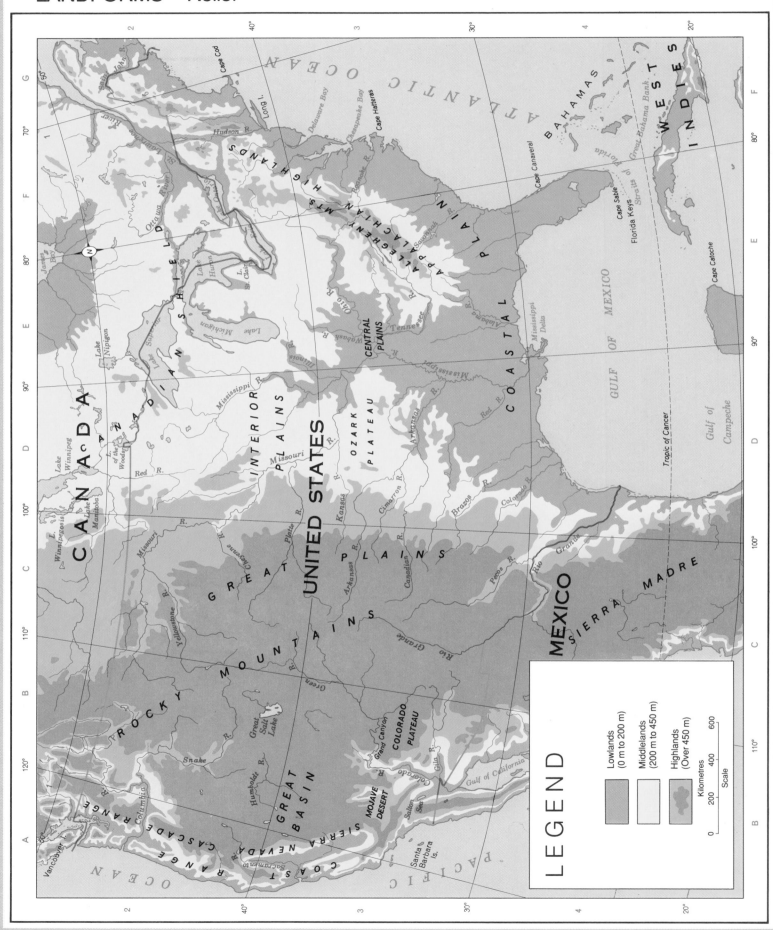

LEGEND

Lowlands
(0 m to 200 m)

Middlelands
(200 m to 450 m)

Highlands
(Over 450 m)

Kilometres

0   200   400   600

Scale

Mexico
POLITICAL DIVISIONS

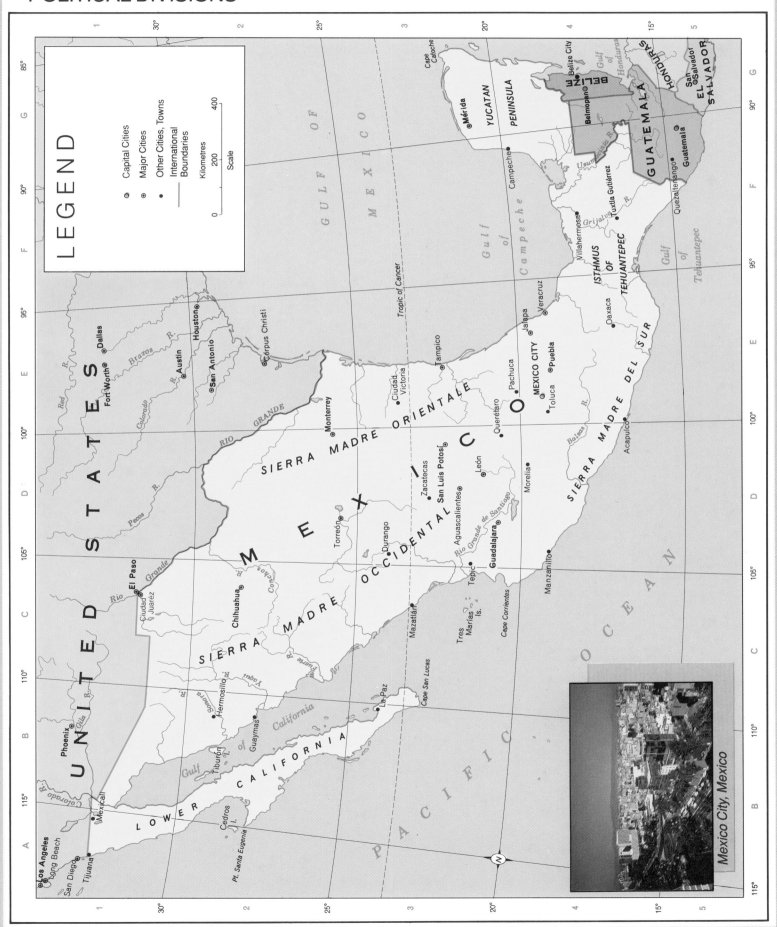

LEGEND

- ⊚ Capital Cities
- ⊙ Major Cities
- • Other Cities, Towns
- — International Boundaries

Kilometres
400
200
0
Scale

UNITED STATES

Los Angeles
Long Beach
San Diego
Tijuana
Mexicali
Phoenix

Dallas
Fort Worth⊙
Austin
San Antonio
Houston⊙
Corpus Christi

Red R.
Brazos R.
Colorado R.
Pecos R.
RIO GRANDE
Rio Grande

El Paso
Ciudad Juárez
Chihuahua⊙

Hermosillo⊙
Guaymas

Gulf of California
Tiburón I.

LOWER CALIFORNIA

La Paz
Cape San Lucas
Pt. Santa Eugenia
Cedros I.

Mazatlán
Tres Marias Is.
Cape Corrientes

SIERRA MADRE OCCIDENTAL

Torreón
Durango
Tepic
Guadalajara⊙

Monterrey⊙

SIERRA MADRE ORIENTALE

Ciudad Victoria
Tampico

Zacatecas
San Luis Potosí⊚
Aguascalientes⊚
León
Querétaro

M E X I C O

Pachuca
MEXICO CITY⊚
Puebla
Toluca
Morelia
Manzanillo
Acapulco

SIERRA MADRE DEL SUR

Jalapa
Veracruz
Oaxaca

Tropic of Cancer

GULF OF MEXICO

Cape Catoche

YUCATAN PENINSULA

Mérida⊚
Campeche

Gulf of Campeche

Villahermosa⊚
Grijalva R.
Tuxtla Gutiérrez⊚

ISTHMUS OF TEHUANTEPEC

Gulf of Tehuantepec

Belize City
Gulf of Honduras
BELIZE
Belmopan⊚
Usumacinta R.

GUATEMALA
HONDURAS
Quezaltenango
Guatemala⊚
San Salvador
EL SALVADOR

PACIFIC OCEAN

N

Mexico City, Mexico

115° 110° 105° 100° 95° 90°
90° 95° 100° 105° 110° 115°

Central America
POLITICAL DIVISIONS

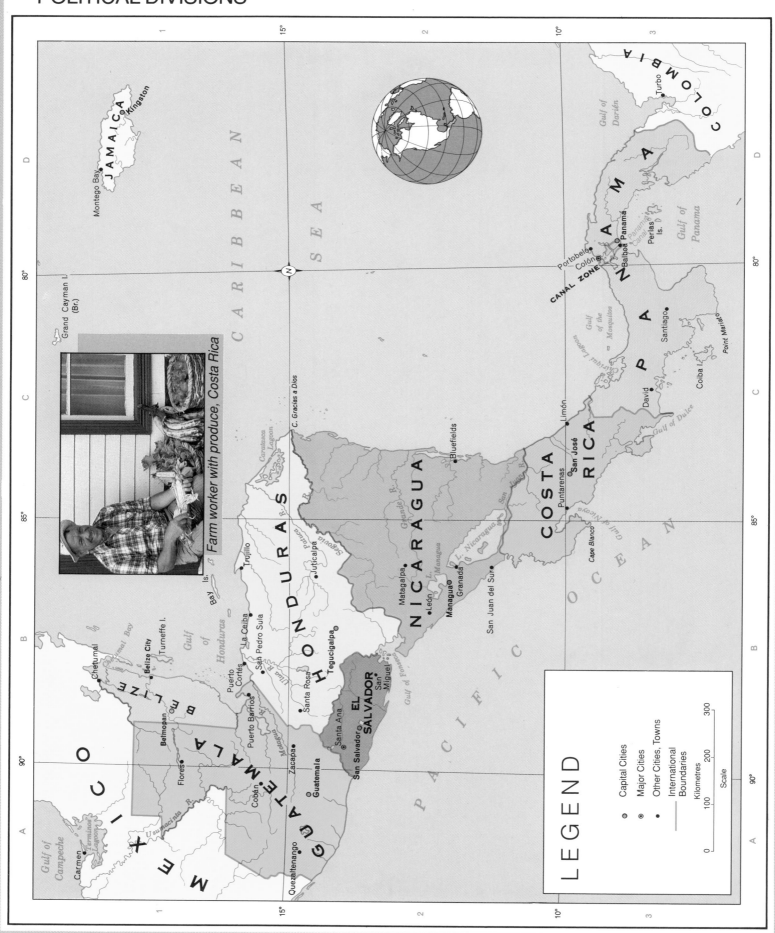

Farm worker with produce, Costa Rica

JAMAICA
Kingston
Montego Bay

Grand Cayman I. (Br.)

C A R I B B E A N   S E A

COLOMBIA
Turbo
Gulf of Darién

P A N A M A
Panamá
Balboa
Portobelo
Colón
CANAL ZONE
Perlas Is. D.
Gulf of Panama
Point María

Santiago
David
Coiba I.

Gulf of the Mosquitos
Chiriqui Lagoon

C. Gracias a Dios

Limón
COSTA RICA
San José
Puntarenas
Gulf of Dulce

Cape Blanco
Gulf of Nicoya

Cariataca Lagoon

H O N D U R A S
Trujillo
Juticalpa
Tegucigalpa

NICARAGUA
Matagalpa
León
Managua
Granada
L. Managua
L. Nicaragua
San Juan R.
Grande R.
Segovia R.
Patuca R.

Bluefields

San Juan del Sur

Bay Is.

La Ceiba
San Pedro Sula
Puerto Cortés
Santa Rosa
Puerto Barrios

BELIZE
Belize City
Belmopan
Chetumal
Turneffe I.
Chetumal Bay
Gulf of Honduras
Ulúa R.
Motagua R.

GUATEMALA
Flores
Cobán
Zacapa
Guatemala
Quezaltenango

EL SALVADOR
Santa Ana
San Salvador
San Miguel
Gulf of Fonseca

MEXICO
Gulf of Campeche
Carmen
Términos Lagoon
Usumacinta R.

P A C I F I C   O C E A N

N

LEGEND
● Capital Cities
◉ Major Cities
• Other Cities, Towns
— International Boundaries

Kilometres
0   100   200   300
Scale

The Caribbean Islands
POLITICAL DIVISIONS

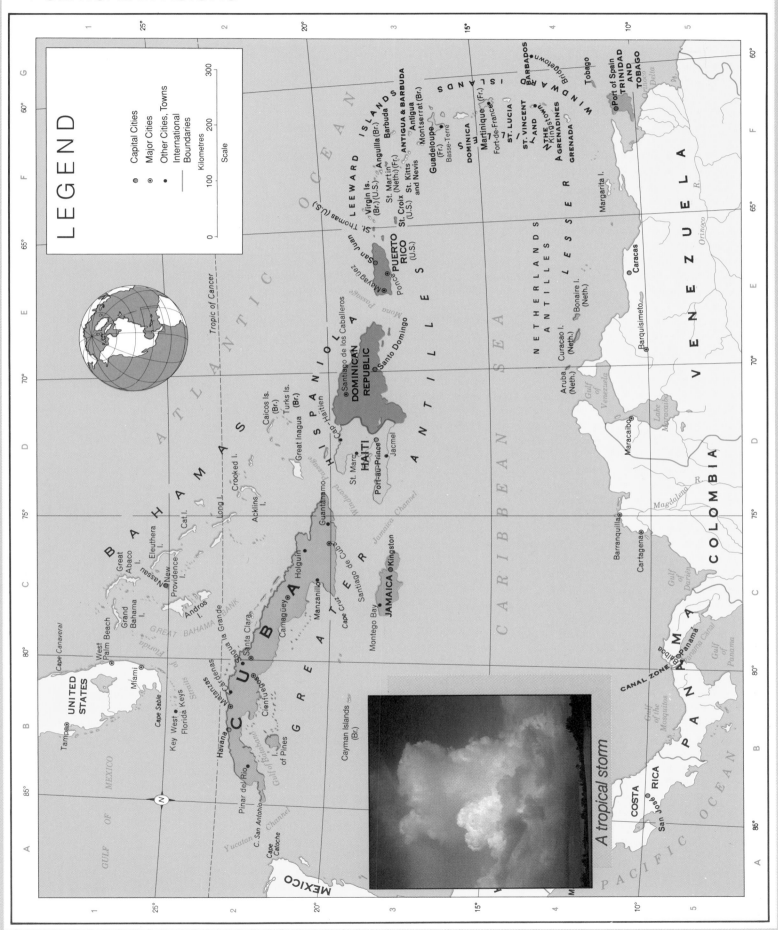

LEGEND

- ● Capital Cities
- ◉ Major Cities
- • Other Cities, Towns
- — International Boundaries

Scale
Kilometres
0   100   200   300

A tropical storm

UNITED STATES

MEXICO

GULF OF MEXICO

Cape Canaveral
Tampa
Miami
West Palm Beach
Key West
Florida Keys
Cape Sable
Pinar del Río
C. San Antonio
Cape Catoche
Yucatan Channel

Strait of Florida

BAHAMAS
Great Abaco I.
Grand Bahama I.
Eleuthera I.
New Providence
Nassau
Andros I.
Cat I.
Long I.
Crooked I.
Acklins I.
GREAT BAHAMA BANK
Cayman Islands (Br.)

CUBA
Havana
Matanzas
Cienfuegos
Santa Clara
Sabana la Grande
Camagüey
Holguín
Manzanillo
Cape Cruz
Guantánamo
Isla de Pines
Gulf of Batabanó

GREATER ANTILLES

JAMAICA
Kingston
Montego Bay
Santiago de Cuba
Jamaica Channel

HISPANIOLA
HAITI
Port-au-Prince
Cap-Haïtien
St. Marc
Jacmel
Caicos Is. (Br.)
Turks Is. (Br.)
Great Inagua I.
Windward Passage

DOMINICAN REPUBLIC
Santiago de los Caballeros
Santo Domingo
Mona Passage

PUERTO RICO (U.S.)
San Juan
Mayagüez
Ponce

Virgin Is. (Br.) (U.S.)
St. Thomas (U.S.)
Anguilla (Br.)
St. Martin (Fr.)
St. Croix (U.S.)
St. Kitts and Nevis

LEEWARD ISLANDS

Barbuda
ANTIGUA & BARBUDA
Antigua
Montserrat (Br.)
Guadeloupe (Fr.)
Basse-Terre
DOMINICA
Martinique (Fr.)
Fort-de-France
ST. LUCIA
ST. VINCENT
Kingstown
THE GRENADINES
GRENADA

WINDWARD ISLANDS

BARBADOS
Bridgetown

LESSER ANTILLES

NETHERLANDS ANTILLES
Curaçao I. (Neth.)
Bonaire I. (Neth.)
Aruba (Neth.)
Margarita I.

TRINIDAD AND TOBAGO
Tobago
Port of Spain

CARIBBEAN SEA

ATLANTIC OCEAN

VENEZUELA
Caracas
Barquisimeto
Maracaibo
Lake Maracaibo
Gulf of Venezuela
Orinoco R.
Orinoco Delta

COLOMBIA
Barranquilla
Cartagena
Magdalena R.
Gulf of Darién

PANAMA
Balboa
Panamá
CANAL ZONE
Panama Canal
Gulf of Panama

COSTA RICA
San José
Gulf of the Mosquitos

PACIFIC OCEAN

Tropic of Cancer

South America
POLITICAL DIVISIONS

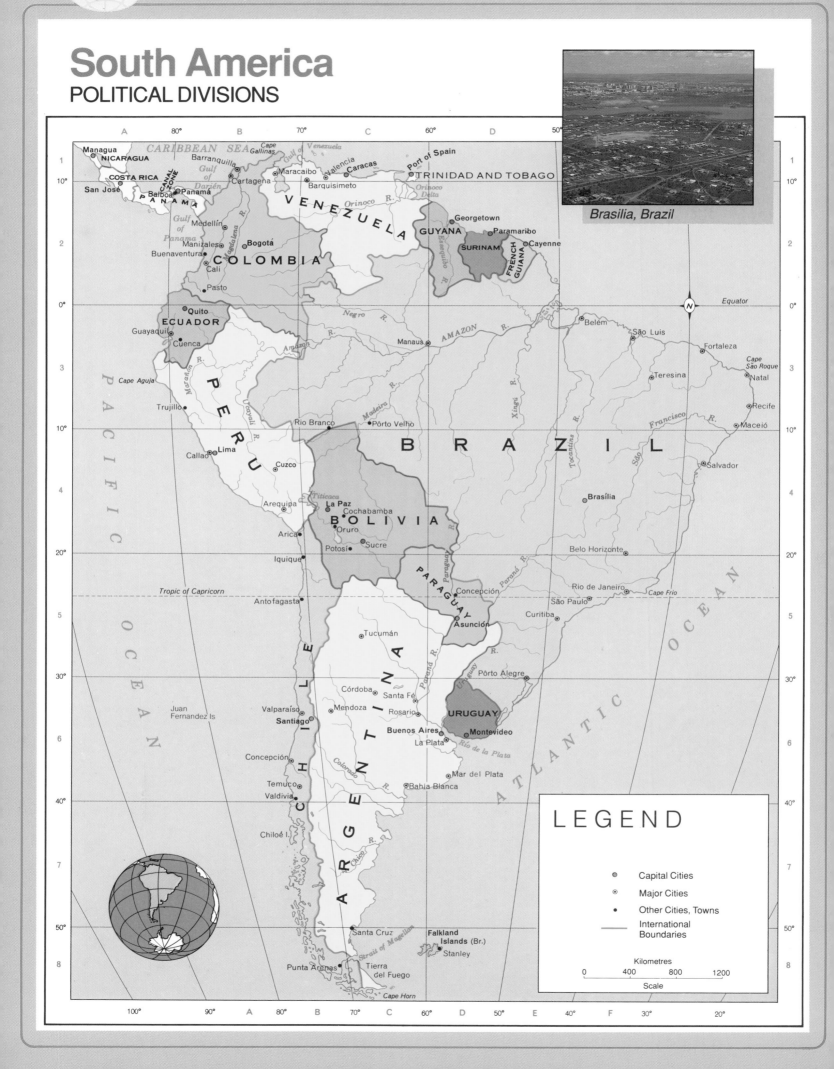

Brasilia, Brazil

NICARAGUA
Managua
COSTA RICA
San José
Balboa
CANAL ZONE
PANAMA
Panamá

CARIBBEAN SEA
Cape Gallinas
Gulf of Darién
Barranquilla
Cartagena
Maracaibo
Valencia
Caracas
Barquisimeto
Port of Spain
TRINIDAD AND TOBAGO
Venezuela
Gulf of Venezuela
Orinoco R.
Orinoco Delta

VENEZUELA

Medellín
Manizales
Bogotá
Buenaventura
Cali
Pasto

COLOMBIA

Georgetown
GUYANA
Paramaribo
SURINAM
Cayenne
FRENCH GUIANA

Quito
ECUADOR
Guayaquil
Cuenca

Negro R.

Equator

Belém
São Luis
Fortaleza
Cape São Roque
Natal

Cape Aguja

PERU

Manaus
AMAZON R.
Teresina

Recife

Trujillo
Rio Branco
Pôrto Velho

Maceió

BRAZIL

Callao
Lima
Cuzco

Arequipa
Titicaca
La Paz
Cochabamba

BOLIVIA

Oruro

Brasília

Arica
Potosí
Sucre

Salvador

Iquique

Belo Horizonte

Tropic of Capricorn

Antofagasta

PARAGUAY

Concepción

Rio de Janeiro
Cape Frio
São Paulo

Tucumán

Asunción

Curitiba

Córdoba
Santa Fé

ARGENTINA

CHILE

Valparaíso
Mendoza
Santiago
Rosario

Pôrto Alegre

URUGUAY

Juan Fernandez Is

Concepción

Buenos Aires
La Plata
Montevideo
Rio de la Plata

Temuco
Valdivia

Mar del Plata
Bahía Blanca

PACIFIC OCEAN

ATLANTIC OCEAN

Chiloé I.

Santa Cruz
Falkland Islands (Br.)
Stanley
Strait of Magellan
Punta Arenas
Tierra del Fuego
Cape Horn

LEGEND

- ⊙ Capital Cities
- ⊙ Major Cities
- • Other Cities, Towns
- — International Boundaries

Kilometres
0   400   800   1200
Scale

South America
LANDFORMS—Relief

CARIBBEAN SEA
Cape Gallinas
Gulf of Darién
Gulf of Panama
Venezuela
Gulf of
Orinoco Delta
TRINIDAD AND TOBAGO
Magdalena R.
Orinoco R.
LLANOS
GUIANA HIGHLANDS
Essequibo R.
Negro R.
Amazon R.
AMAZON
Cape Agúja
Marañón R.
Ucayali R.
SELVAS
Madeira R.
Cape São Roque
A N D E S
L. Titicaca
Xingú R.
Tocantins R.
Francisco
São
R.
MATO GROSSO UPLAND
PLATEAU OF BOLIVIA
Tropic of Capricorn
GRAN CHACO
Paraguay R.
Paraná R.
BRAZILIAN HIGHLANDS
Cape Frio
Juan Fernandez Is
Uruguay
CAMPOS
Paraná R.
Colorado R.
PAMPAS
Río de la Plata
Chiloé I.
Chiloé
CHONOS ARCHIPELAGO
P A T A G O N I A
PACIFIC OCEAN
ATLANTIC OCEAN
Equator
Strait of Magellan
Falkland Islands (Br.)
Tierra del Fuego
Cape Horn

LEGEND

	Lowlands (0 m to 200 m)
	Middlelands (200 m to 450 m)
	Highlands (Over 450 m)

Kilometres
0   400   800   1200
Scale

South America
TEMPERATURES—January and July

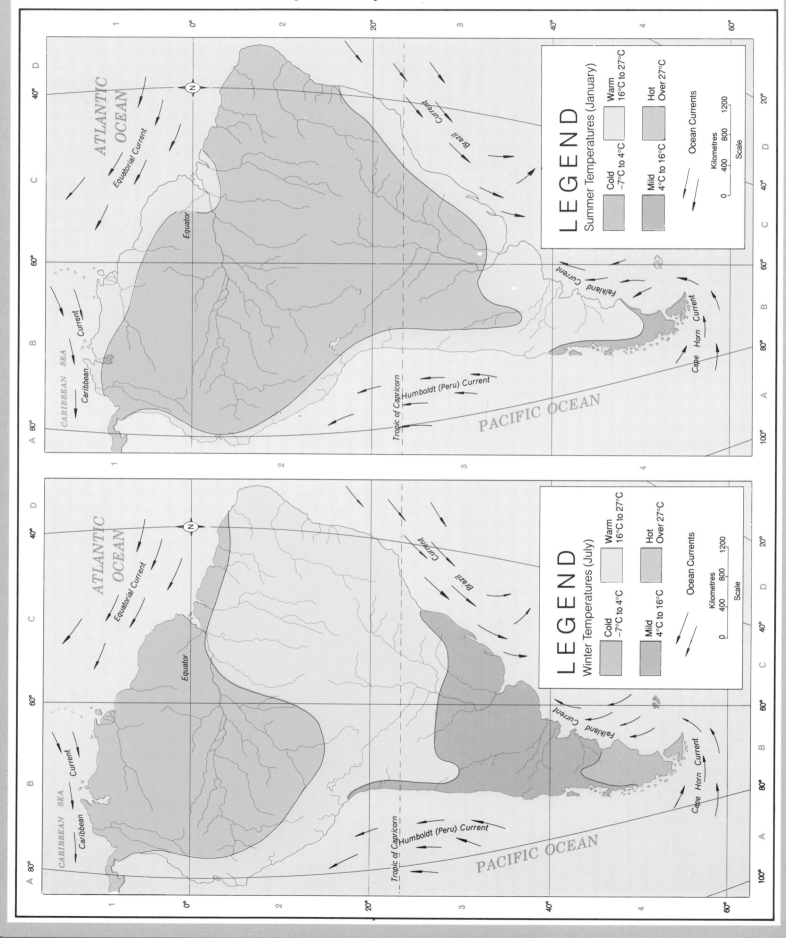

South America
ANNUAL RAINFALL and VEGETATION

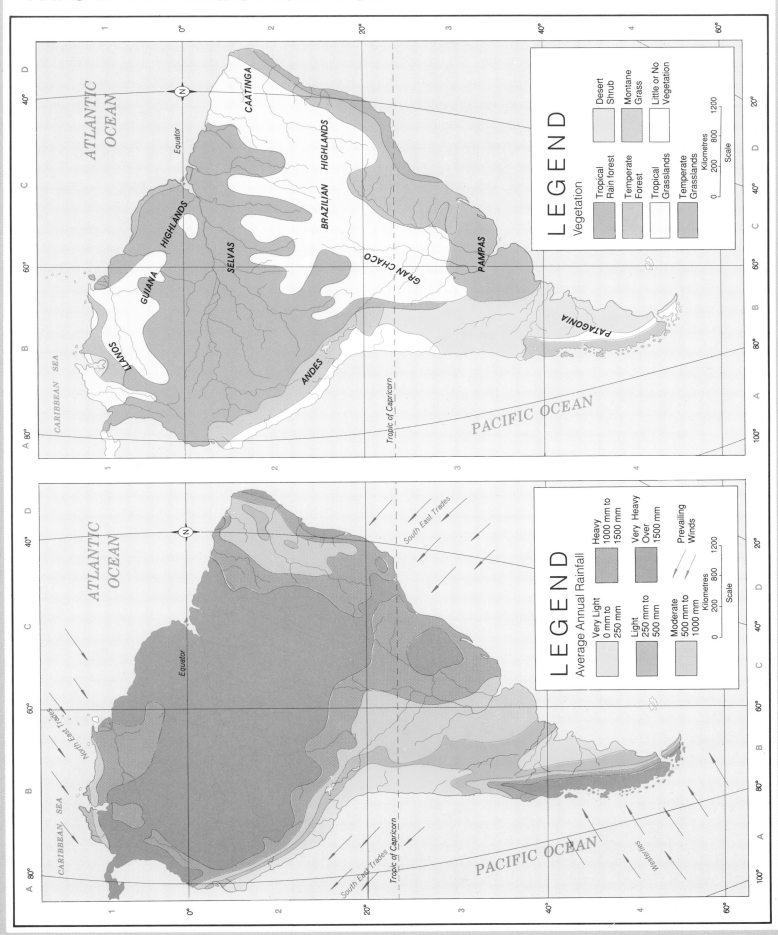

LEGEND
Vegetation

- Tropical Rain forest
- Temperate Forest
- Tropical Grasslands
- Temperate Grasslands
- Desert Shrub
- Montane Grass
- Little or No Vegetation

Kilometres
Scale
0   200   400   800   1200

LEGEND
Average Annual Rainfall

- Very Light 0 mm to 250 mm
- Light 250 mm to 500 mm
- Moderate 500 mm to 1000 mm
- Heavy 1000 mm to 1500 mm
- Very Heavy Over 1500 mm
- Prevailing Winds

Kilometres
Scale
0   200   400   800   1200

South America
RAIN FORESTS

South American rain forests, before and after clearing

Where Our Rain Forests Go

Somewhere in the world, 12 to 20 hectares of rain forest disappear every thirty minutes. Forty percent of the world's rain forests have already vanished. By the year 2000, some countries will have lost their entire forest area.

Yanomami Indians in the Amazon rain forest.

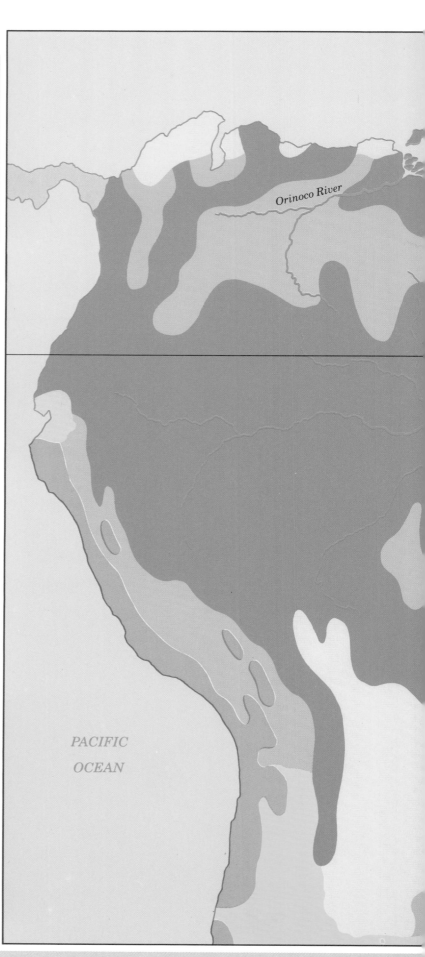

Orinoco River

PACIFIC OCEAN

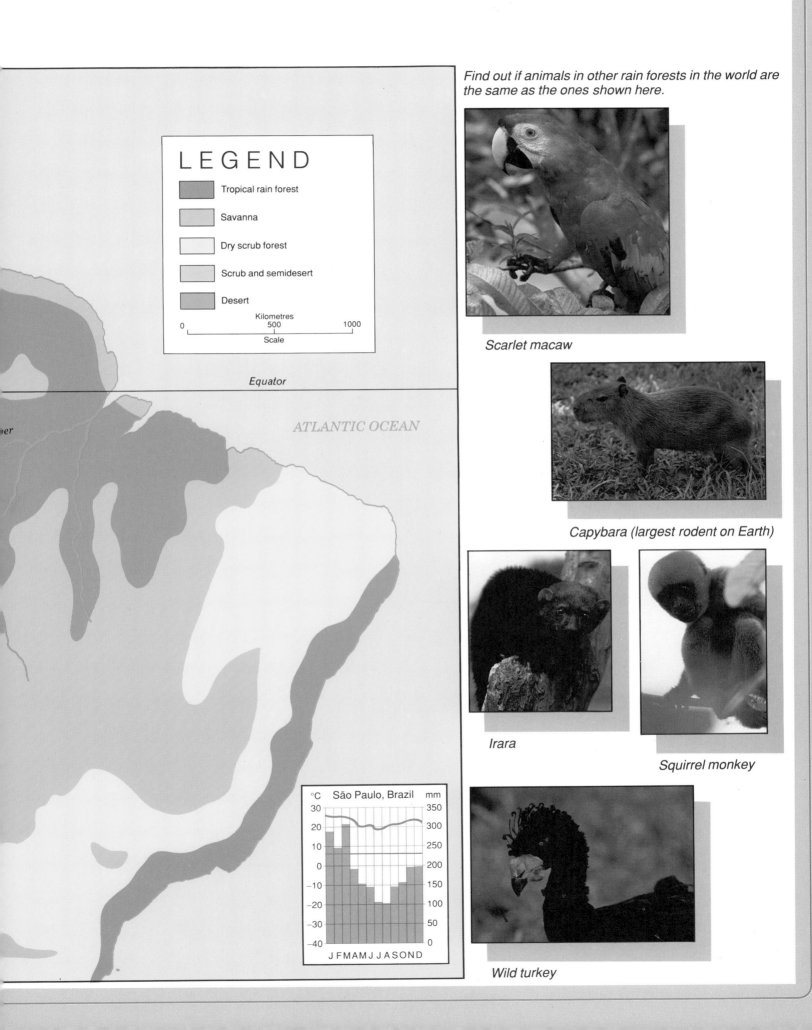

LEGEND

- Tropical rain forest
- Savanna
- Dry scrub forest
- Scrub and semidesert
- Desert

Kilometres
0   500   1000
Scale

Equator

ATLANTIC OCEAN

°C São Paulo, Brazil mm

J F M A M J J A S O N D

Find out if animals in other rain forests in the world are the same as the ones shown here.

Scarlet macaw

Capybara (largest rodent on Earth)

Irara

Squirrel monkey

Wild turkey

Africa
POLITICAL DIVISIONS

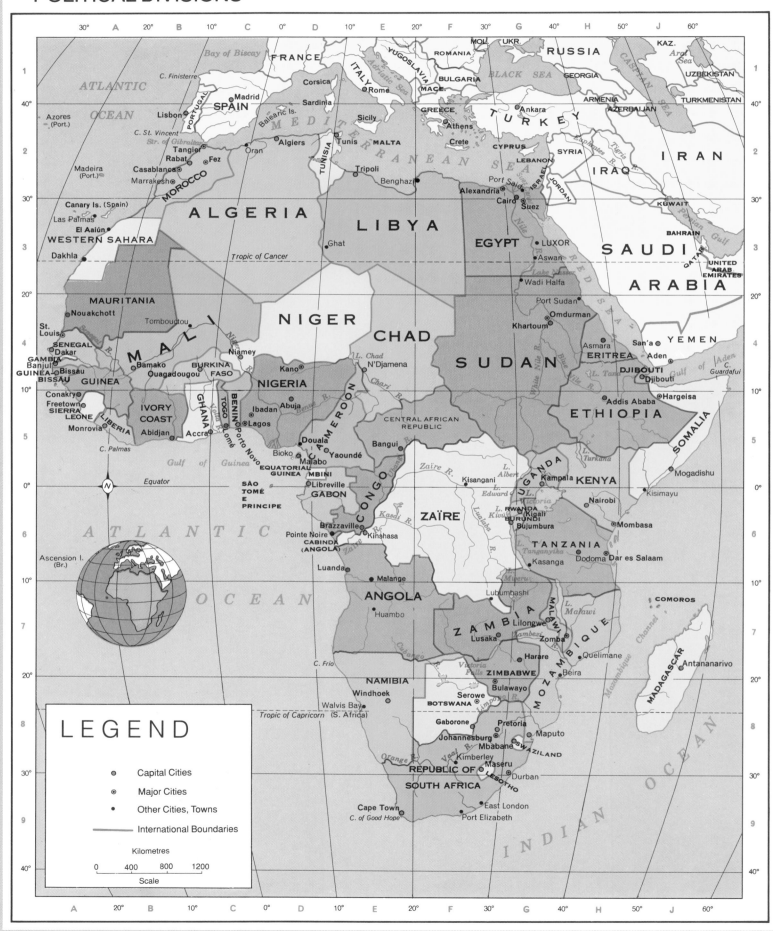

LEGEND

- ⊙ Capital Cities
- ⊗ Major Cities
- • Other Cities, Towns
- — International Boundaries

Kilometres

0   400   800   1200

Scale

Nairobi, Kenya

Cape Town, South Africa

Luxor, Egypt

Algiers, Algeria

Africa
LANDFORMS—Relief

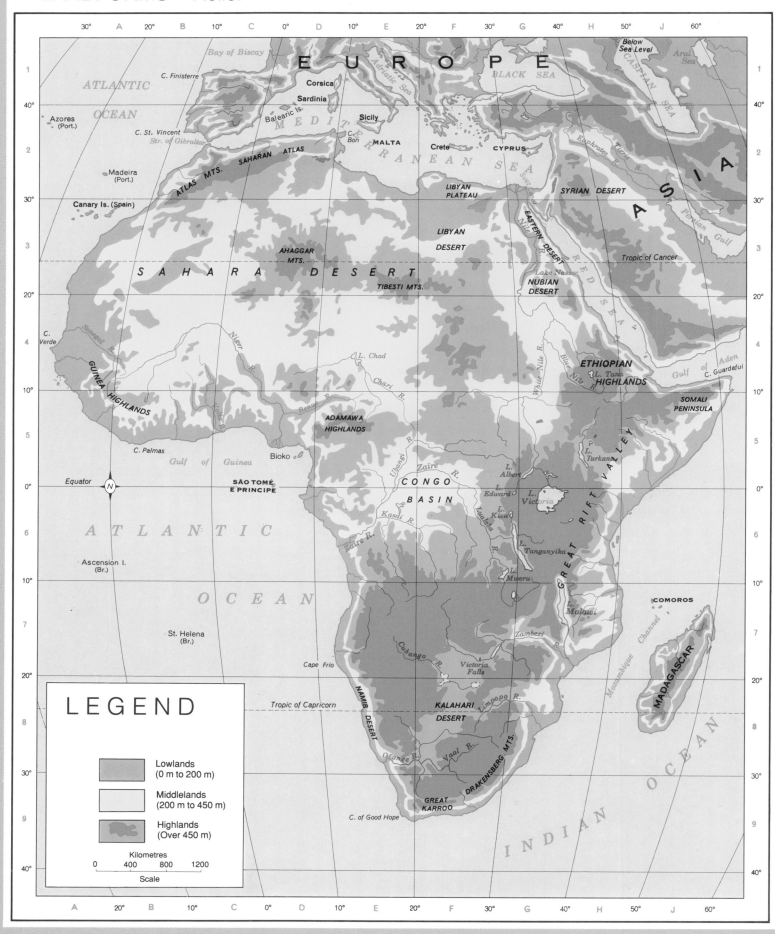

EUROPE

ASIA

ATLANTIC OCEAN

Bay of Biscay

C. Finisterre

Corsica

Sardinia

Balearic Is.

Sicily

MALTA

Crete

CYPRUS

Adriatic Sea

BLACK SEA

Below Sea Level

CASPIAN SEA

Aral Sea

Azores (Port.)

Madeira (Port.)

C. St. Vincent
Str. of Gibraltar

ATLAS MTS.

SAHARAN ATLAS

C. Bon

MEDITERRANEAN SEA

LIBYAN PLATEAU

SYRIAN DESERT

Euphrates R.
Tigris R.

Canary Is. (Spain)

AHAGGAR MTS.

LIBYAN DESERT

EASTERN DESERT

Suez Canal

Nile

Persian Gulf

Tropic of Cancer

SAHARA DESERT

TIBESTI MTS.

Lake Nasser

NUBIAN DESERT

RED SEA

C. Verde

Senegal R.

Niger R.

L. Chad

Chari R.

White Nile R.

Blue Nile R.

L. Tana

ETHIOPIAN HIGHLANDS

Gulf of Aden

C. Guardafui

GUINEA HIGHLANDS

Benue R.

Volta R.

ADAMAWA HIGHLANDS

SOMALI PENINSULA

C. Palmas

Bioko

Gulf of Guinea

SÃO TOMÉ E PRINCIPE

Equator

N

Ubangi R.

Zaire R.

CONGO BASIN

Kasai R.

L. Albert

L. Edward

L. Kivu

L. Victoria

L. Turkana

GREAT RIFT VALLEY

Zaire R.

Lualaba R.

L. Tanganyika

L. Mweru

ATLANTIC

OCEAN

Ascension I. (Br.)

St. Helena (Br.)

L. Malawi

COMOROS

Zambezi R.

Cubango R.

Victoria Falls

Cape Frio

NAMIB DESERT

KALAHARI DESERT

Limpopo R.

Tropic of Capricorn

MADAGASCAR

Mozambique Channel

Orange R.

Vaal R.

DRAKENSBERG MTS.

GREAT KARROO

C. of Good Hope

INDIAN OCEAN

LEGEND

Lowlands (0 m to 200 m)	
Middlelands (200 m to 450 m)	
Highlands (Over 450 m)	

Kilometres

0   400   800   1200

Scale

Desert Record

The Sahara desert is the largest desert in the world with an area of over 8 million square kilometres. It grows larger every year.

Sun and Sand Facts

The eastern Sahara region is the sunniest place in the world. It has over 4 300 h of sunshine each year.

East central Algeria has the highest sand dunes in the world. The highest dunes measure 430 m.

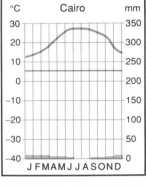

Sahara, Niger

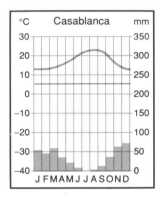

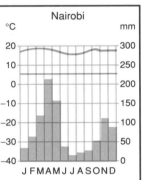

Cameroon

Foothills, Ethiopia

River Facts

The longest river in the world runs through the largest desert area in the world. This river is called the Nile River.

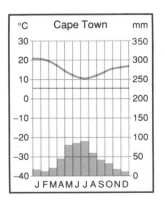

Hex River Valley, South Africa

Europe
POLITICAL DIVISIONS

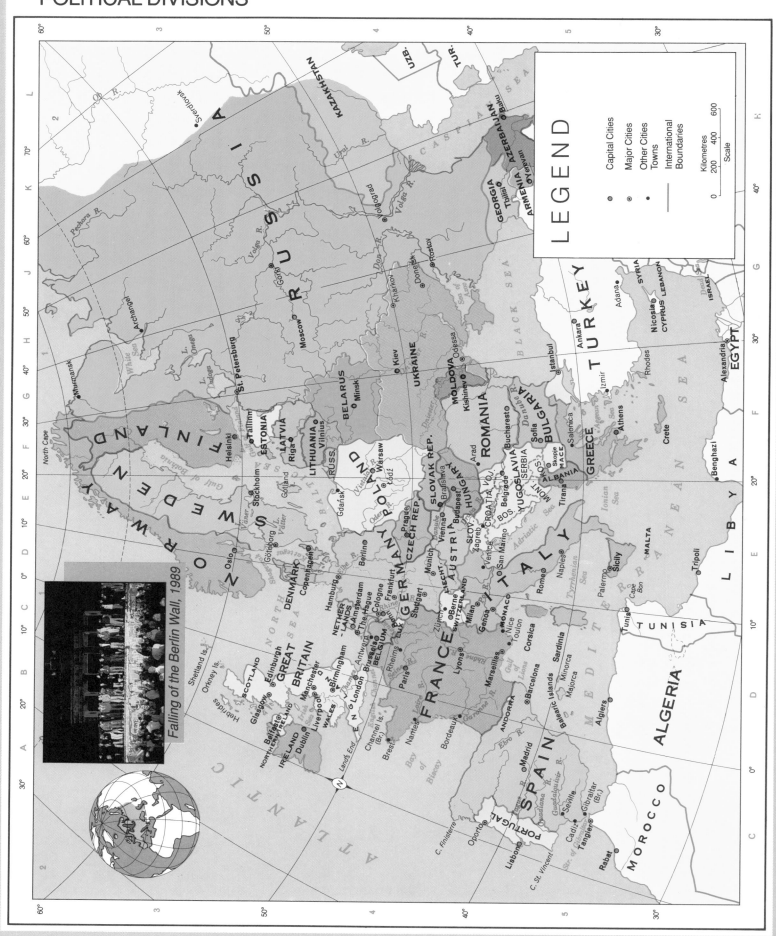

LEGEND

- Capital Cities
- Major Cities
- Other Cities
- Towns
- International Boundaries

Kilometres
0   200   400   600
Scale

Falling of the Berlin Wall, 1989

Europe
LANDFORMS—Relief

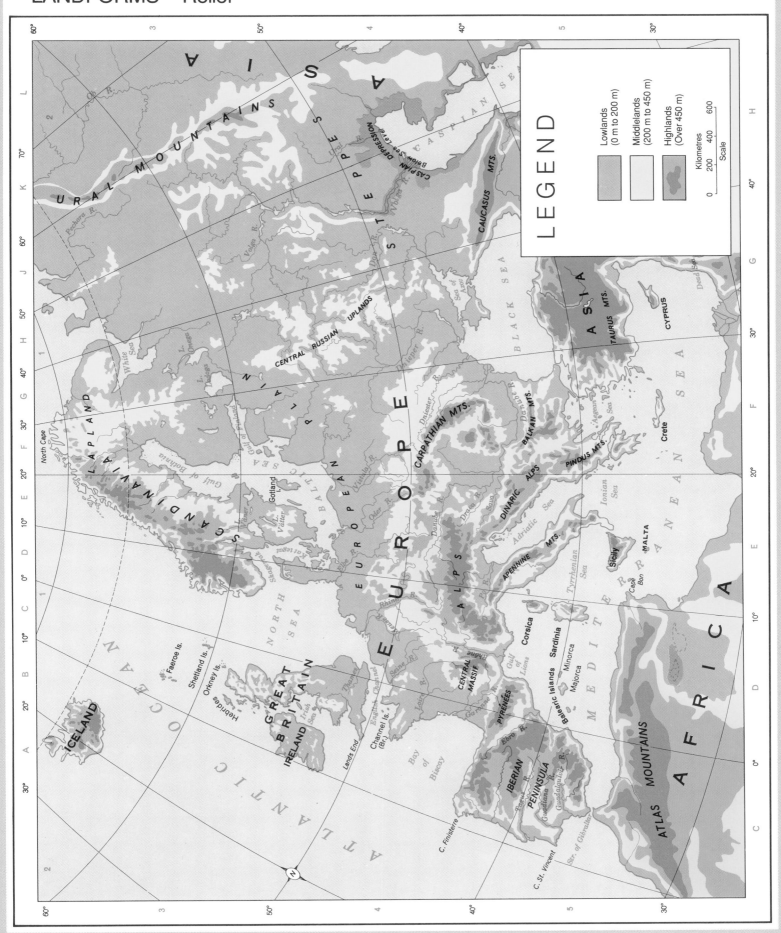

LEGEND

Lowlands
(0 m to 200 m)

Middlelands
(200 m to 450 m)

Highlands
(Over 450 m)

Kilometres
0   200   400   600
Scale

ASIA

URAL MOUNTAINS

Ob R.

Pechora R.

Volga R.

Don R.

Ural R.

CASPIAN DEPRESSION
Below Sea Level

CASPIAN SEA

STEPPE

CAUCASUS MTS.

CENTRAL RUSSIAN UPLANDS

L. Onega

L. Ladoga

White Sea

LAPLAND

SCANDINAVIA

North Cape

Gulf of Bothnia

Dnieper R.

Dniester R.

Don R.

Sea of Azov

BLACK SEA

ASIA

TAURUS MTS.

CYPRUS

Dead Sea

CARPATHIAN MTS.

Danube R.

BALKAN MTS.

PINDUS MTS.

DINARIC ALPS

Aegean Sea

Crete

Ionian Sea

EUROPEAN PLAIN

Vistula R.

Oder R.

Elbe R.

Danube R.

Drave R.

Save R.

ALPS

APENNINE MTS.

Adriatic Sea

Tyrrhenian Sea

MALTA

Sicily

Corsica

Sardinia

Cape Bon

MEDITERRANEAN SEA

Gotland

L. Vänern

L. Vättern

Skagerrak

Kattegat

BALTIC SEA

Rhine R.

NORTH SEA

GREAT BRITAIN

IRELAND

Irish Sea

Hebrides

Orkney Is.

Shetland Is.

Faeroe Is.

ICELAND

ATLANTIC OCEAN

Lands End

Thames R.

English Channel

Channel Is. (Br.)

Bay of Biscay

C. Finisterre

Seine R.

Loire R.

CENTRAL MASSIF

Rhône R.

Gulf of Lions

Garonne R.

PYRÉNÉES

Ebro R.

IBERIAN PENINSULA

Tagus R.

Guadiana R.

Guadalquivir R.

C. St. Vincent

Str. of Gibraltar

Balearic Islands

Minorca

Majorca

ATLAS MOUNTAINS

AFRICA

EUROPE

N

Asia
POLITICAL DIVISIONS

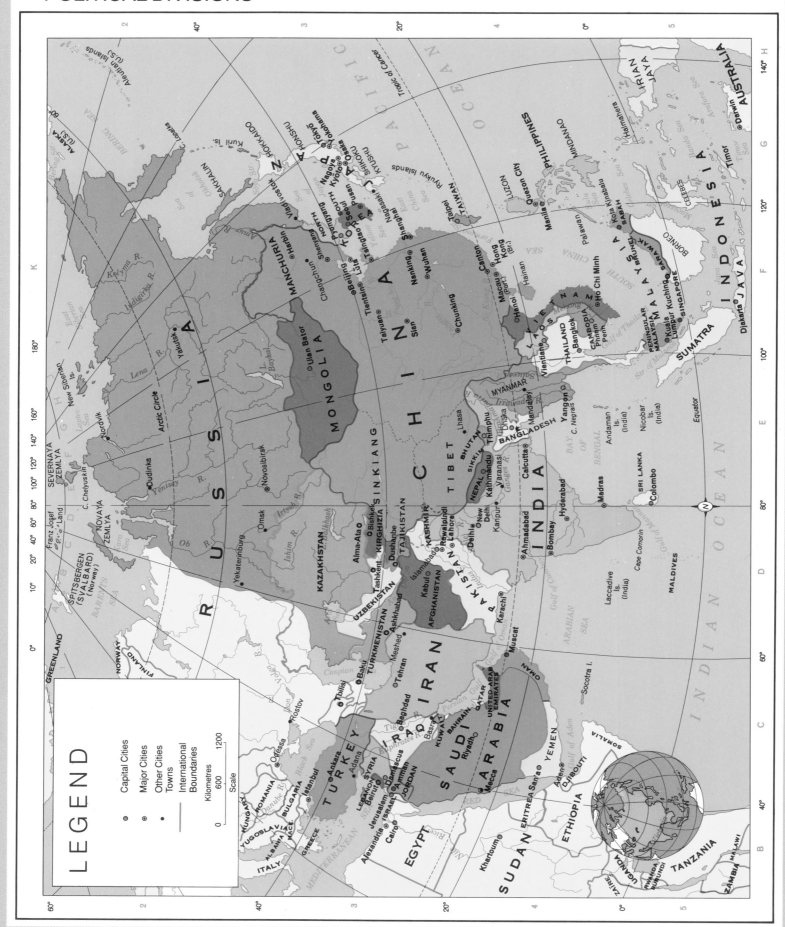

LEGEND

- Capital Cities
- Major Cities
- Other Cities
- Towns
— International Boundaries

Kilometres

0   600   1200

Scale

Asia
LANDFORMS—Relief

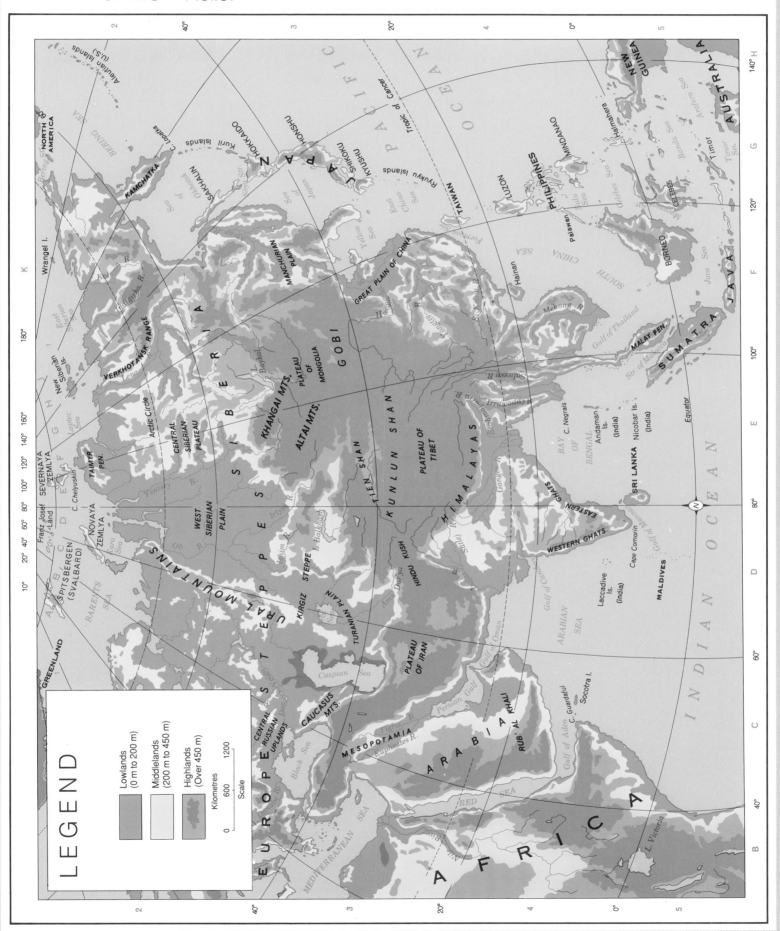

LEGEND

Lowlands (0 m to 200 m)
Middlelands (200 m to 450 m)
Highlands (Over 450 m)

Scale

Kilometres

0   600   1200

Pacific Rim

China

Philippines

ARCTIC OCEAN

RUSSIA

ALASKA (U.S.)

Anchorage

BERING SEA

Sea of Okhotsk

KAZAKHSTAN

MONGOLIA

Vladivostok

Portland
Seattle
Va

UZB.
KIRGHIZIA
TUR.
TAJIKISTAN

Beijing

NORTH KOREA

JAPAN

San Francisc

AFGHANISTAN
PAKISTAN

CHINA

Seoul
SOUTH KOREA

Tokyo
Osaka

Los A

NEPAL
BHUTAN

Shanghai

BANGLADESH

INDIA

MYANMAR

Taipei
TAIWAN

Hawaii (U.S.)

Honolulu

Bombay

LAOS

HONG KONG (U.K.)

Northern Mariana Islands (U.S.)

ARABIAN SEA

BAY OF BENGAL

THAILAND
KAMPUCHEA
VIETNAM

CHINA SEA

Manila
PHILIPPINES

Guam (U.S.)

MARSHALL ISLANDS

international date line

PACIFIC OCEAN

SRI LANKA

BRUNEI

Palau (U.S.)

MALAYSIA
SINGAPORE
BORNEO

EQUATOR

CELEBES

Nauru

Kiribati

Jakarta

INDONESIA

PAPUA NEW GUINEA

Solomon Is.

Tokelau (N.Z.)

Tuvalu

INDIAN OCEAN

Vanuatu

Wallis and Futuna (France)

W. Samoa

Am. Samoa (U.S.)

French Polynesia (France)

Fiji

Cook Islands (N.Z.)

New Caledonia (Fr.)

Tonga

Niue (N.Z.)

Pitca

AUSTRALIA

Brisbane

Sydney

TASMAN SEA

Melbourne

New Zealand

Tasmania

Kerguelen I. (Fr.)

LEGE

○ Capital Cities

• Principal Cities

Kilomet

0   500

Scale

Antarctica

Canada

Main Languages of the Rim

Country	Language Spoken
Argentina	Spanish
Chile	Spanish
Peru	Spanish
Ecuador	Spanish
Colombia	Spanish
Panama	Spanish
Costa Rica	Spanish
Nicaragua	Spanish
El Salvador	Spanish
Guatemala	Spanish
Mexico	Spanish
United States	English
Canada	English, French
Russia	Russian
China	Chinese
Japan	Japanese
Korea	Korean
Vietnam	Vietnamese, French
Indonesia	Bahasa, Indonesian
Malaysia	Malay, Chinese
Philippines	Tagalog, English
New Guinea	Papuan
Australia	English
New Zealand	English

Within each country, many native languages and dialects exist.

Mexico

Ecuador

Australasia
POLITICAL DIVISIONS

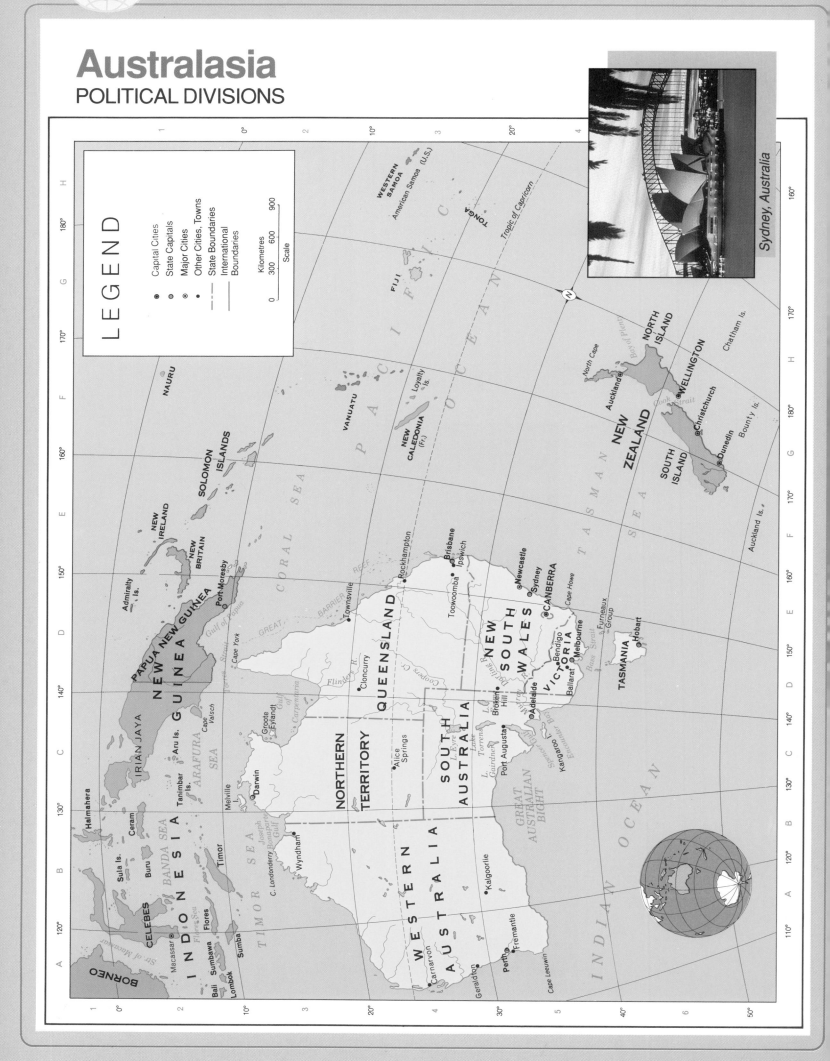

Sydney, Australia

LEGEND

- Capital Cities
- State Capitals
- Major Cities
- Other Cities, Towns
- State Boundaries
- International Boundaries

Kilometres
0   300   600   900
Scale

BORNEO

CELEBES

Macassar
Sula Is.
Buru
Ceram
BANDA SEA
Halmahera

INDONESIA

Flores Sea
Bali
Lombok
Sumbawa
Sumba
Flores
Timor
Tanimbar Is.
Aru Is.
Cape Valsch
IRIAN JAYA

Str. of Macassar

PAPUA NEW GUINEA

NEW GUINEA

Admiralty Is.

NEW IRELAND

NEW BRITAIN

Port Moresby

SOLOMON ISLANDS

NAURU

VANUATU

NEW CALEDONIA (Fr.)

Loyalty Is.

FIJI

TONGA

WESTERN SAMOA

American Samoa (U.S.)

Tropic of Capricorn

P A C I F I C   O C E A N

C O R A L   S E A

Gulf of Papua
Torres Strait
Cape York
GREAT
BARRIER
REEF

TIMOR SEA

ARAFURA SEA

Gulf of Carpentaria

C. Londonderry
Joseph Bonaparte Gulf

Melville
Darwin
Melville Is.
Groote Eylandt

Wyndham

WESTERN AUSTRALIA

NORTHERN TERRITORY

QUEENSLAND

Alice Springs

Flinders R.
Cloncurry
Townsville
Rockhampton

Cooper's Cr.

Brisbane
Ipswich
Toowoomba

SOUTH AUSTRALIA

L. Eyre
L. Torrens
L. Gairdner

Port Augusta
Broken Hill
Adelaide

NEW SOUTH WALES

Newcastle
Sydney
CANBERRA
Cape Howe

Darling R.
Murray R.

VICTORIA
Bendigo
Ballarat
Melbourne

Kangaroo I.
Spencer Gulf
Encounter Bay

Carnarvon
Geraldton
Perth
Fremantle
Cape Leeuwin
Kalgoorlie

GREAT AUSTRALIAN BIGHT

Cape Leeuwin

INDIAN OCEAN

Furneaux Group
Bass Strait
King I.

TASMANIA
Hobart

TASMAN SEA

NEW ZEALAND

North Cape
Auckland
NORTH ISLAND
Bay of Plenty
WELLINGTON
Cook Strait
SOUTH ISLAND
Christchurch
Dunedin
Bounty Is.
Chatham Is.

Auckland Is.

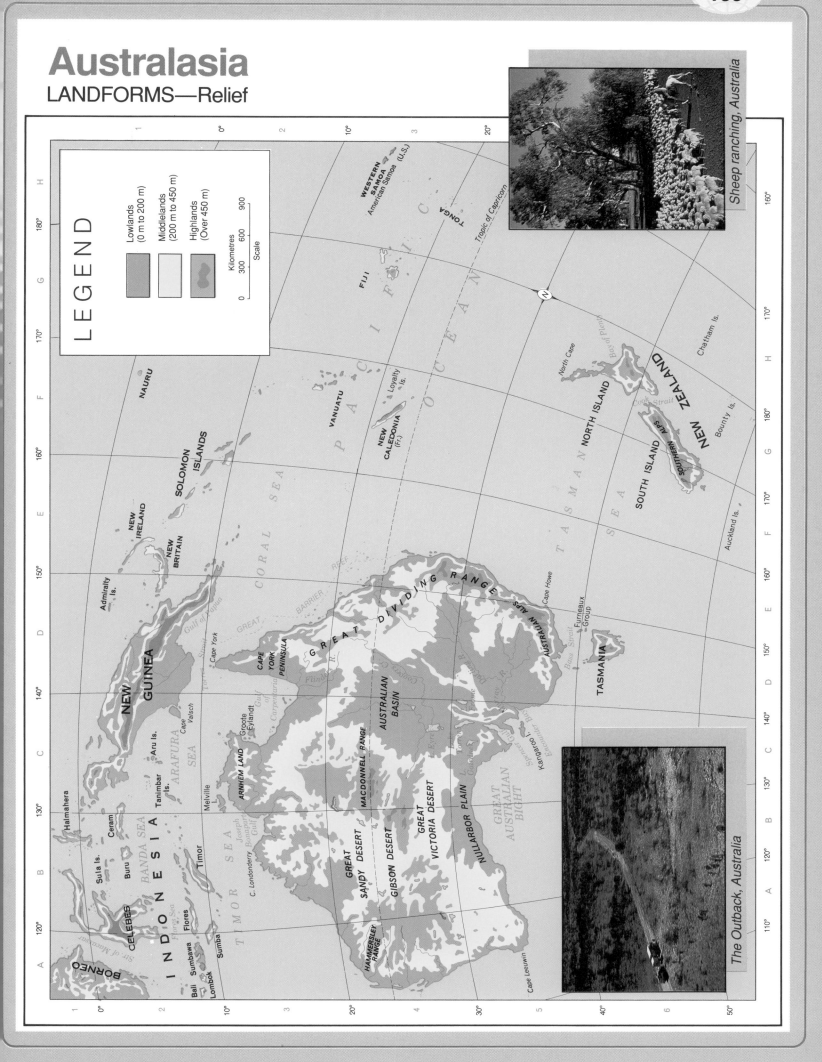

Australasia
LANDFORMS—Relief

LEGEND

Lowlands (0 m to 200 m)
Middlelands (200 m to 450 m)
Highlands (Over 450 m)

Kilometres
0 300 600 900
Scale

Sheep ranching, Australia

The Outback, Australia

Antarctica

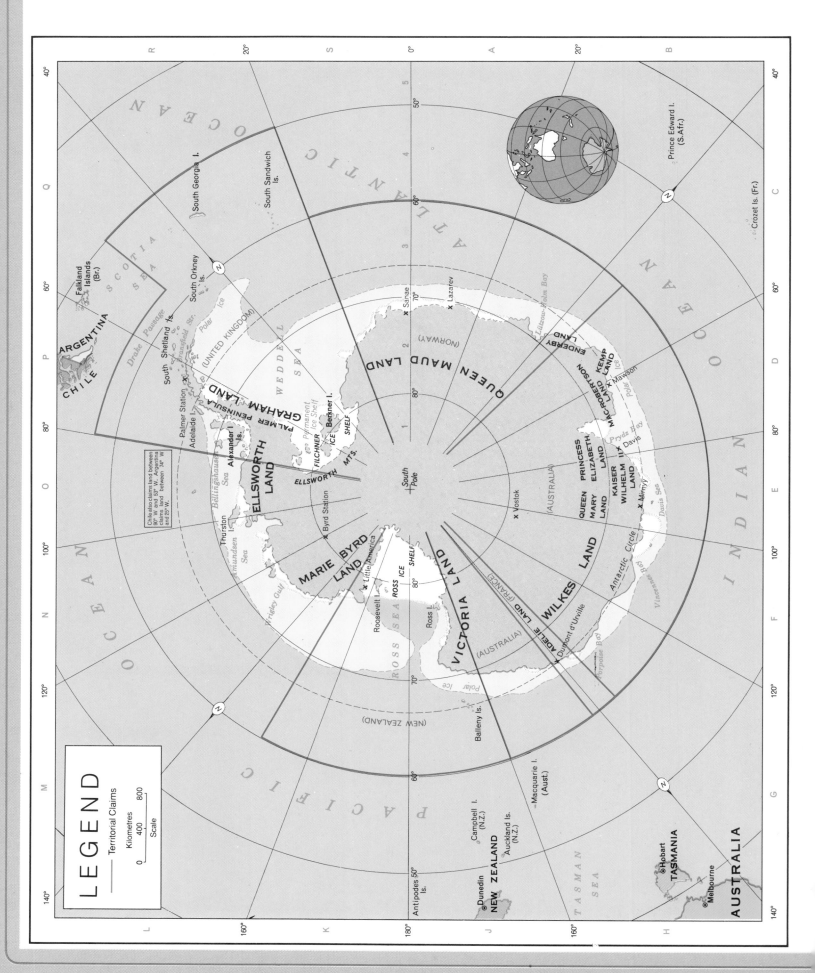

110

Ozone Facts

The damaging ultra-violet rays which come from the sun are absorbed by a layer of ozone high above Earth. In recent years, scientists have discovered that this layer over the poles has grown thinner than it once was. Between 1979 and 1986, the average global ozone levels dropped by 5 percent.

Penguins, Antarctica

Antarctic Research Station

The Arctic

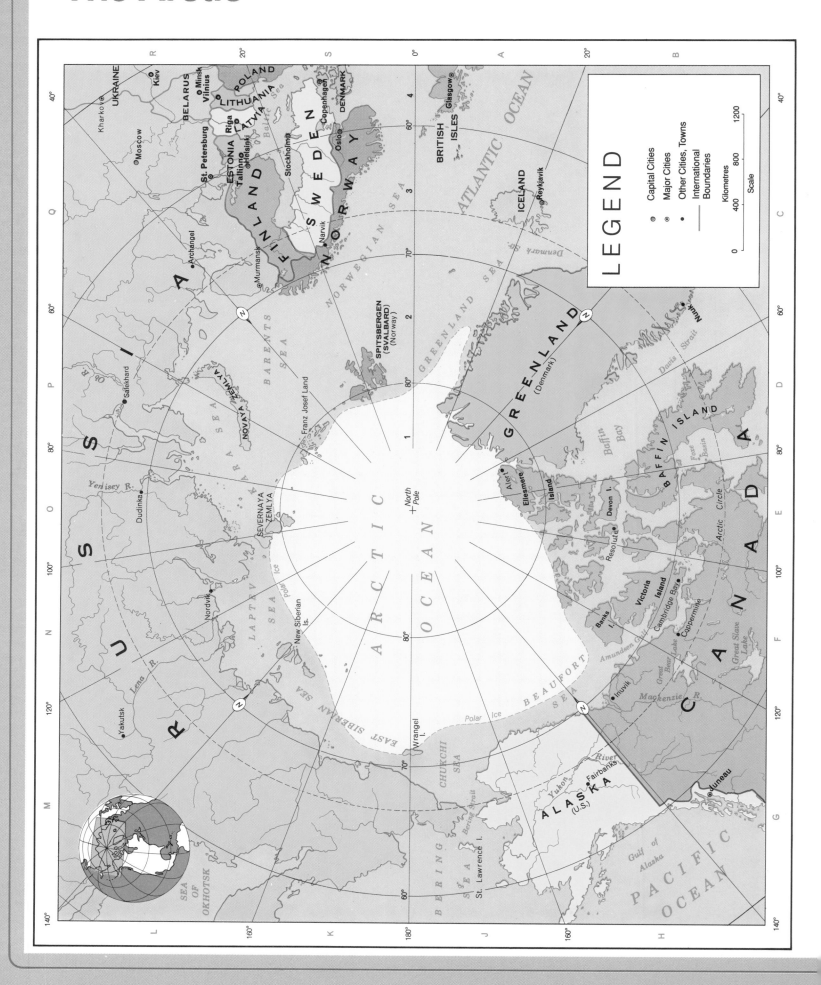

LEGEND

- Capital Cities
- Major Cities
- Other Cities, Towns
- International Boundaries

Kilometres
0 400 800 1200
Scale

UKRAINE
Kharkov
Kiev
BELARUS
Minsk
Vilnius
LITHUANIA
POLAND
Riga
LATVIA
Moscow
ESTONIA
Tallinn
Helsinki
St. Petersburg
Copenhagen
DENMARK
Stockholm
SWEDEN
NORWAY
Oslo
Narvik
FINLAND
Archangel
Murmansk

BRITISH ISLES
Glasgow
ATLANTIC OCEAN
ICELAND
Reykjavik

NORWEGIAN SEA
BARENTS SEA
SPITSBERGEN (SVALBARD) (Norway)
Franz Josef Land
GREENLAND SEA
Denmark Str.

R U S S I A
Salekhard
NOVAYA ZEMLYA
KARA SEA
SEVERNAYA ZEMLYA
Yenisey R.
Dudinka
Ob R.
LAPTEV SEA
Nordvik
Lena R.
New Siberian Is.
Polar Ice
EAST SIBERIAN SEA
Yakutsk
Wrangel I.
CHUKCHI SEA
Bering Strait

ARCTIC OCEAN
North Pole

GREENLAND (Denmark)
Nuuk
Alert
Ellesmere Island
Baffin Bay
Davis Strait
Devon I.
Resolute
BAFFIN ISLAND
Foxe Basin
Arctic Circle
Victoria Island
Cambridge Bay
Banks I.
Coppermine
Amundsen Gulf
Great Bear Lake
Great Slave Lake
Mackenzie R.
Inuvik
BEAUFORT SEA
Polar Ice
C A N A D A
Yukon River
Fairbanks
ALASKA (U.S.)
Juneau
Gulf of Alaska
PACIFIC OCEAN

BERING SEA
St. Lawrence I.
SEA OF OKHOTSK

Walrus, The Arctic

Seals, The Arctic

The North West Territories

World Exploration

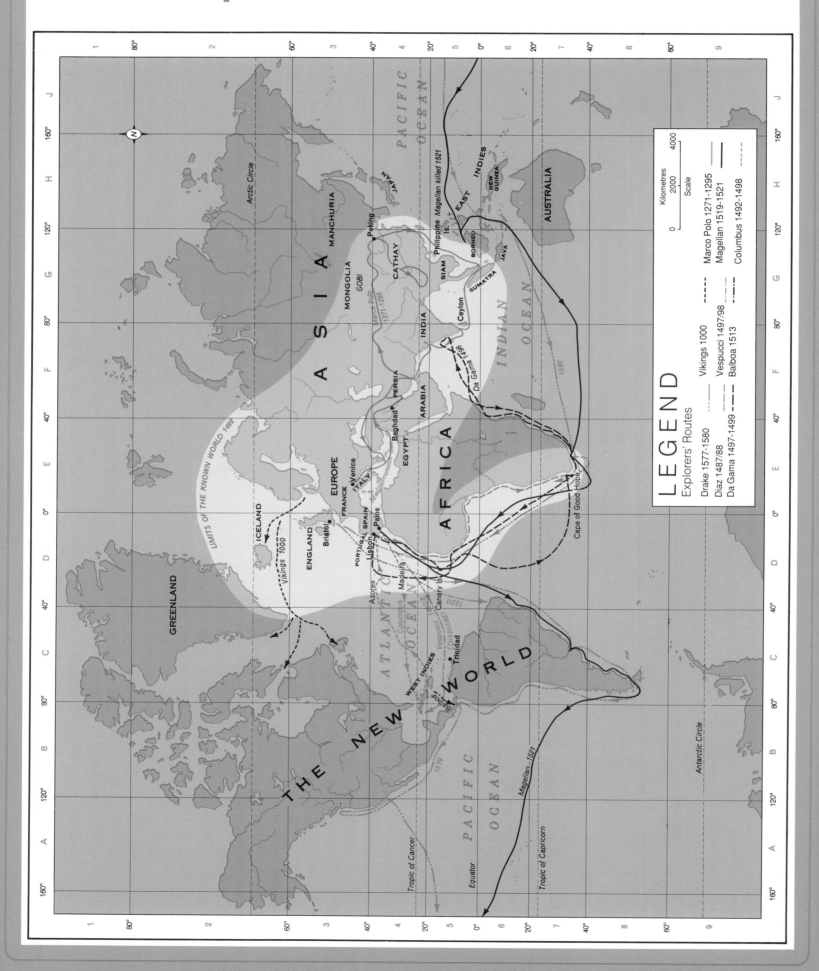

Explorers

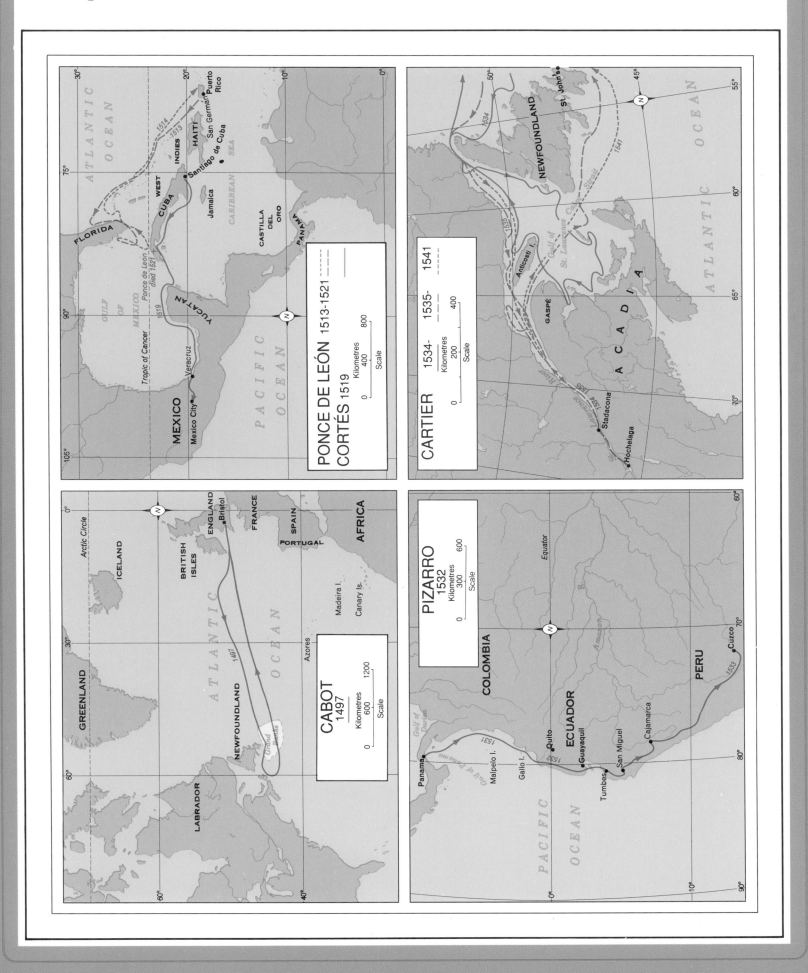

Explorers

PONCE DE LEÓN 1513–1521
CORTÉS 1519

Ponce de León died 1521

ATLANTIC OCEAN — WEST INDIES — FLORIDA — CUBA — HAITI — San Germán — Puerto Rico — Santiago de Cuba — Jamaica — CARIBBEAN SEA — CASTILLA DEL ORO — PANAMA — YUCATAN — GULF OF MEXICO — MEXICO — Mexico City — Veracruz — Tropic of Cancer — PACIFIC OCEAN

Scale
Kilometres
0   400   800

CARTIER 1534– 1535– 1541

NEWFOUNDLAND — St. John's — Gulf of St. Lawrence — Cabot Strait — Anticosti I. — ACADIA — GASPÉ — Stadacona — Hochelaga — St. Lawrence River — ATLANTIC OCEAN

Scale
Kilometres
0   200   400

CABOT 1497

Arctic Circle — GREENLAND — ICELAND — BRITISH ISLES — ENGLAND — Bristol — FRANCE — SPAIN — PORTUGAL — AFRICA — Madeira I. — Canary Is. — Azores — ATLANTIC OCEAN — NEWFOUNDLAND — Grand Banks — LABRADOR

Scale
Kilometres
0   600   1200

PIZARRO 1532

COLOMBIA — Equator — Gulf of Darien — Panama — Malpelo I. — Gallo I. — Quito — ECUADOR — Guayaquil — Tumbes — San Miguel — Cajamarca — Amazon R. — PERU — Cuzco — PACIFIC OCEAN

Scale
Kilometres
0   300   600

Explorers

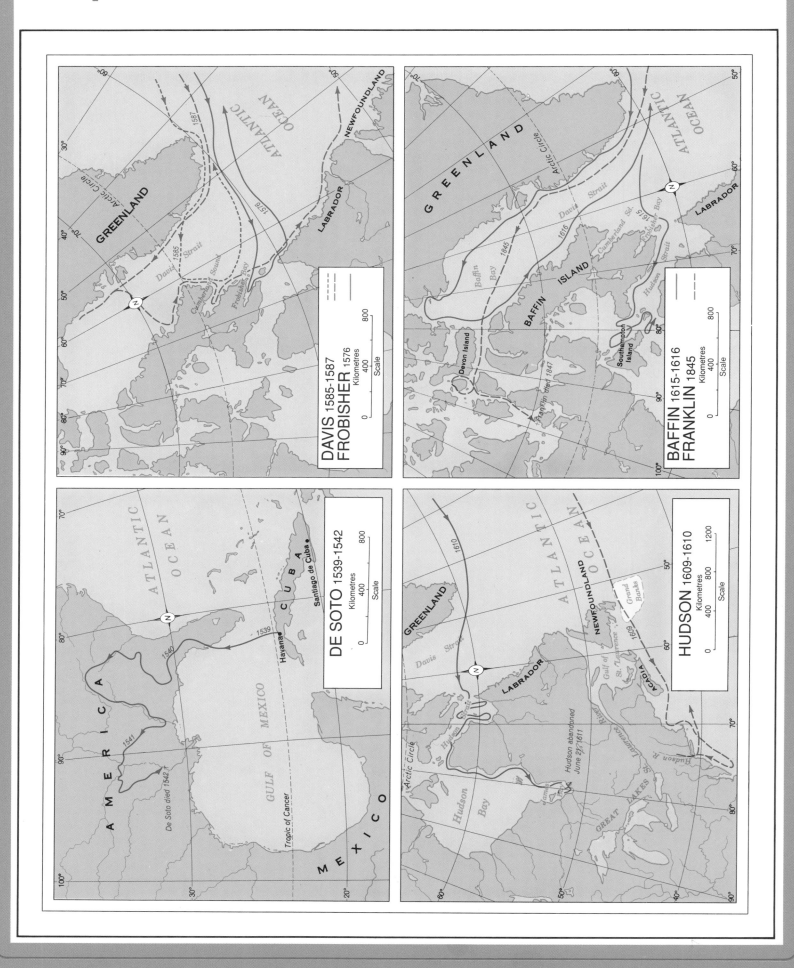

Explorers

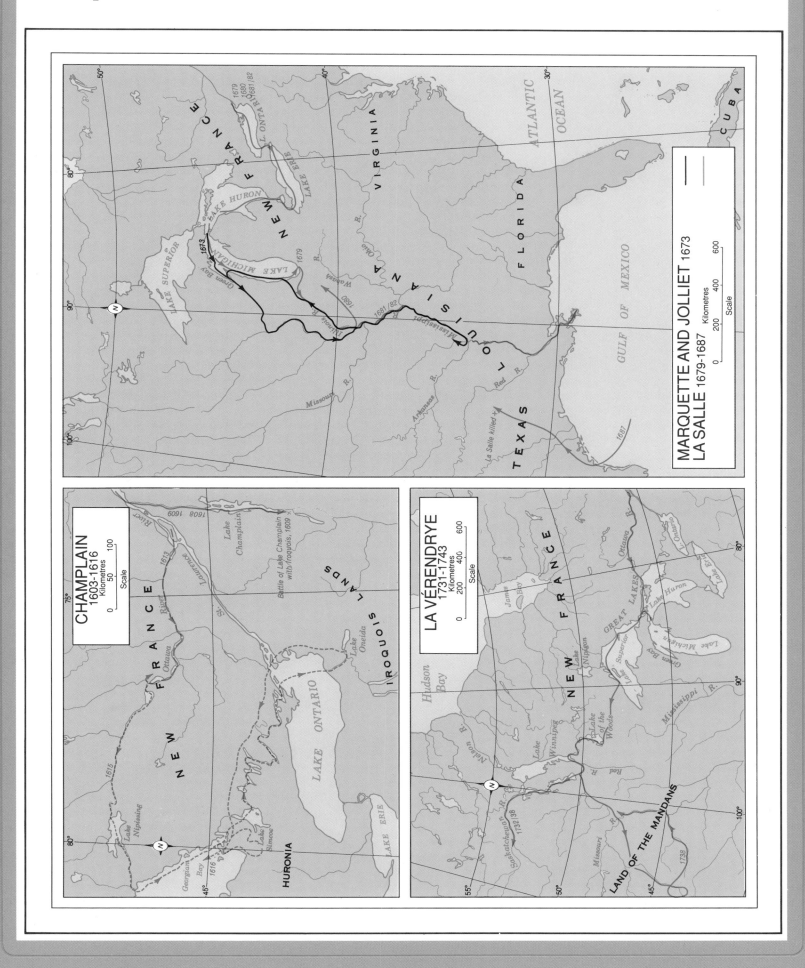

MARQUETTE AND JOLLIET 1673
LA SALLE 1679-1687

Kilometres
Scale
0   200   400   600

NEW FRANCE

LAKE SUPERIOR

Lake Huron

LAKE MICHIGAN

LAKE ERIE

L. ONTARIO

Green Bay

Illinois R.

Wabash R.

Ohio R.

Mississippi R.

Missouri R.

Arkansas R.

Red R.

LOUISIANA

VIRGINIA

FLORIDA

TEXAS

CUBA

ATLANTIC OCEAN

GULF OF MEXICO

La Salle killed

1673 1679 1680 1681/82 1687

CHAMPLAIN 1603-1616

Kilometres
Scale
0   50   100

NEW FRANCE

Ottawa River

St. Lawrence River

Lake Champlain

Battle of Lake Champlain with Iroquois, 1609

IROQUOIS LANDS

LAKE ONTARIO

LAKE ERIE

HURONIA

Lake Nipissing

Georgian Bay

Lake Simcoe

1608 1609 1613 1615 1616

LA VÉRENDRYE 1731-1743

Kilometres
Scale
0   200   400   600

Hudson Bay

James Bay

NEW FRANCE

GREAT LAKES

Lake Superior

Lake Michigan

Green Bay

Lake Huron

Lake Nipigon

Lr. Ontario

Lake Erie

Ottawa R.

Mississippi R.

Lake Winnipeg

Lake of the Woods

Nelson R.

Saskatchewan R.

Red R.

Missouri R.

LAND OF THE MANDANS

1732/38 1738

Explorers

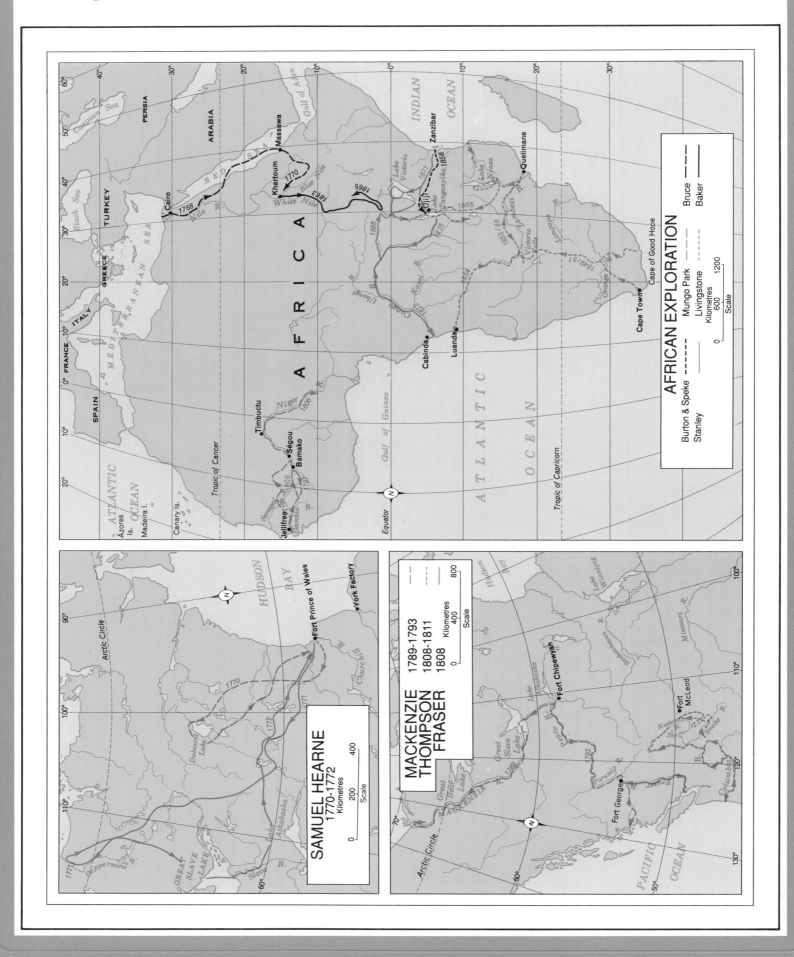

AFRICAN EXPLORATION

Burton & Speke	— — —	Mungo Park	— · — · —
Stanley	————	Livingstone	· · · · · ·
		Bruce	– – –
		Baker	————

Scale
Kilometres
0   600   1200

SAMUEL HEARNE
1770-1772

Scale
Kilometres
0   200   400

MACKENZIE   1789-1793
THOMPSON   1808-1811
FRASER   1808

Scale
Kilometres
0   400   800

Polar Exploration

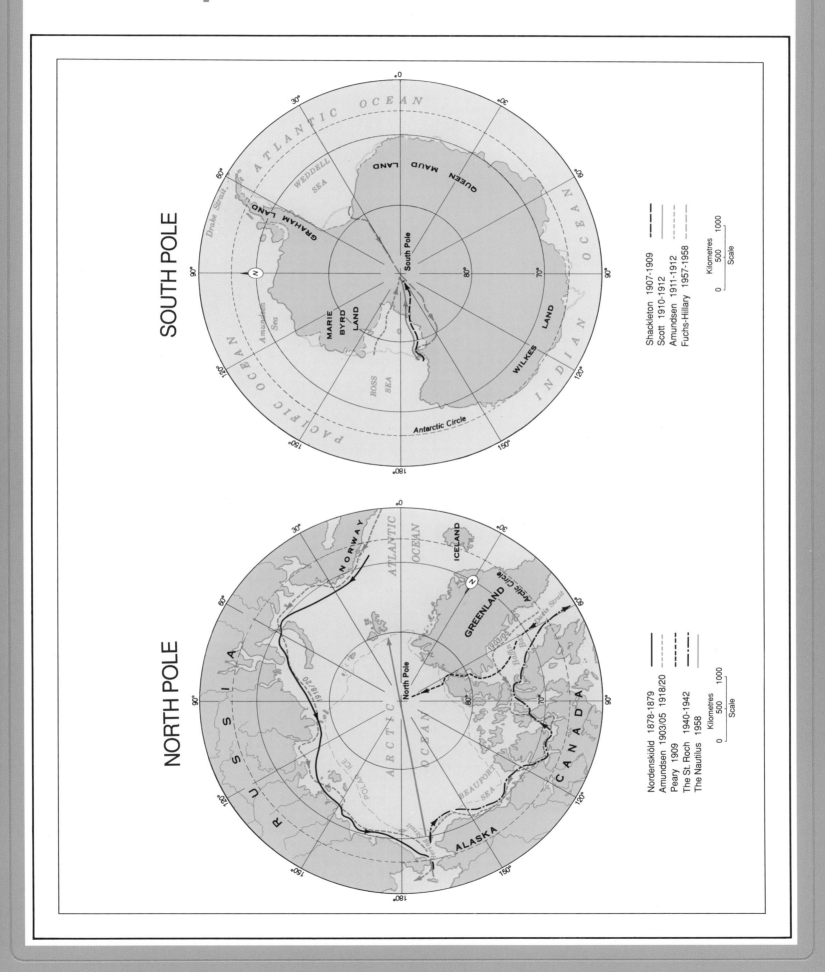

SOUTH POLE

Shackleton 1907-1909
Scott 1910-1912
Amundsen 1911-1912
Fuchs-Hillary 1957-1958

Kilometres
0 500 1000
Scale

NORTH POLE

Nordenskiöld 1878-1879
Amundsen 1903/05 1918/20
Peary 1909
The St. Roch 1940-1942
The Nautilus 1958

Kilometres
0 500 1000
Scale

North America
NATIVE PEOPLES—1500

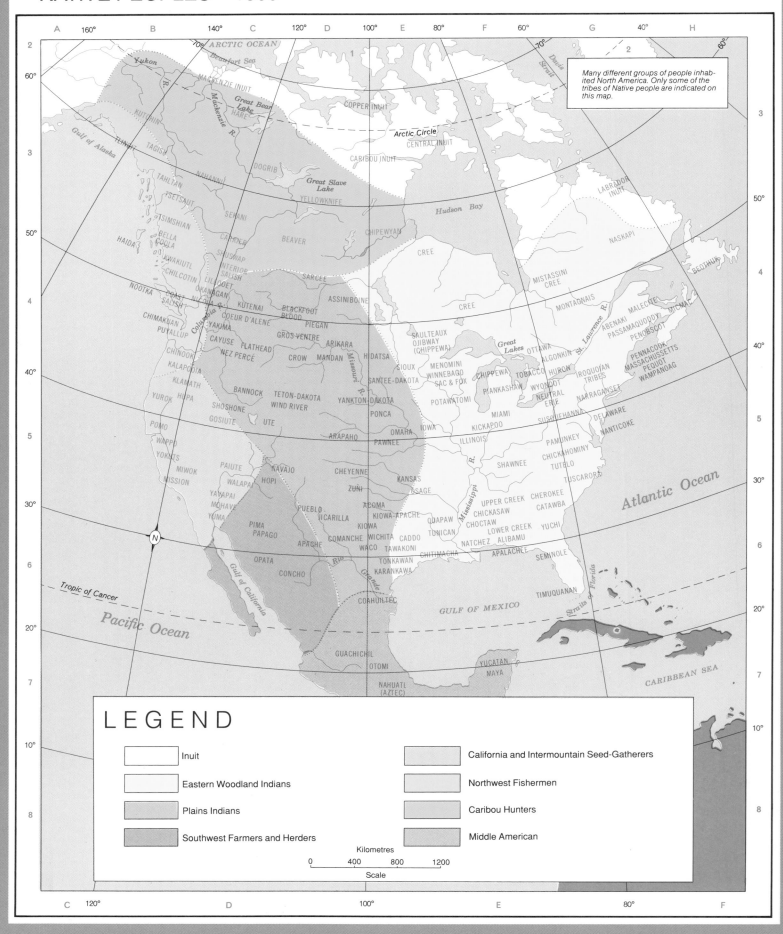

Many different groups of people inhabited North America. Only some of the tribes of Native people are indicated on this map.

ARCTIC OCEAN
Beaufort Sea
Yukon
MACKENZIE INUIT
Great Bear Lake
KUTCHIN
HARE
Mackenzie R.
COPPER INUIT
Arctic Circle
CENTRAL INUIT
TLINGIT
TAGISH
Gulf of Alaska
DOGRIB
CARIBOU INUIT
NAHANNI
TAHLTAN
YSETSAUT
Great Slave Lake
YELLOWKNIFE
LABRADOR INUIT
TSIMSHIAN
SEKANI
Hudson Bay
BELLA COOLA
CARRIER
CHIPEWYAN
HAIDA
SHUSWAP
BEAVER
NASKAPI
KWAKIUTL
INTERIOR SALISH
CREE
CHILCOTIN
LILLOOET
SARCEE
NOOTKA
OKANAGAN
MISTASSINI CREE
NISGA'A
KUTENAI
ASSINIBOINE
BEOTHUK
COAST SALISH
Columbia R.
BLACKFOOT
CREE
MONTAGNAIS
CHIMAKUAN
COEUR D'ALENE
BLOOD
St. Lawrence R.
MALECITE
PUYALLUP
YAKIMA
PIEGAN
MICMAC
CAYUSE
GROS VENTRE
SAULTEAUX
ABENAKI
CHINOOK
PLATHEAD
ARIKARA
OJIBWAY (CHIPPEWA)
OTTAWA
PASSAMAQUODDY
NEZ PERCÉ
CROW
MANDAN
HIDATSA
ALGONKIN
PENOBSCOT
KALAPOOIA
Great Lakes
HURON
PENNACOOK
KLAMATH
SIOUX
MENOMINI
CHIPPEWA
TOBACCO
IROQUOIAN TRIBES
MASSACHUSSETTS
YUROK
HUPA
Missouri R.
WINNEBAGO
WYONDOT
PEQUOT
BANNOCK
TETON-DAKOTA
SANTEE-DAKOTA
SAC & FOX
NEUTRAL
NARRAGANSET
WAMPANOAG
POMO
SHOSHONE
WIND RIVER
YANKTON-DAKOTA
PIANKASHAW
ERIE
GOSIUTE
UTE
PONCA
POTAWATOMI
MIAMI
SUSQUEHANNA
DELAWARE
WAPPO
ARAPAHO
OMAHA
IOWA
KICKAPOO
NANTICOKE
YOKUTS
PAWNEE
ILLINOIS
PAMUNKEY
MIWOK
PAIUTE
NAVAJO
CHEYENNE
R.
SHAWNEE
CHICKAHOMINY
MISSION
WALAPAI
HOPI
KANSAS
TUTELO
YAVAPAI
ZUÑI
OSAGE
Mississippi
UPPER CREEK
CHEROKEE
TUSCARORA
MOHAVE
ACOMA
CATAWBA
YUMA
PUEBLO
JICARILLA
KIOWA-APACHE
CHICKASAW
PIMA
KIOWA
QUAPAW
CHOCTAW
YUCHI
PAPAGO
APACHE
COMANCHE
WICHITA
CADDO
TUNICA
LOWER CREEK
OPATA
WACO
TAWAKONI
NATCHEZ
ALIBAMU
CONCHO
Rio Grande
TONKAWAN
CHITIMACHA
APALACHEE
SEMINOLE
KARANKAWA
Gulf of California
COAHUILTEC
GULF OF MEXICO
Straits of Florida
Atlantic Ocean
TIMUQUANAN
Tropic of Cancer
Pacific Ocean
GUACHICHIL
OTOMI
YUCATAN
MAYA
CARIBBEAN SEA
NAHUATL (AZTEC)

Davis Strait

LEGEND

Inuit	California and Intermountain Seed-Gatherers
Eastern Woodland Indians	Northwest Fishermen
Plains Indians	Caribou Hunters
Southwest Farmers and Herders	Middle American

Kilometres

0   400   800   1200

Scale

Canada
LIFESTYLES OF NATIVE PEOPLES—1500

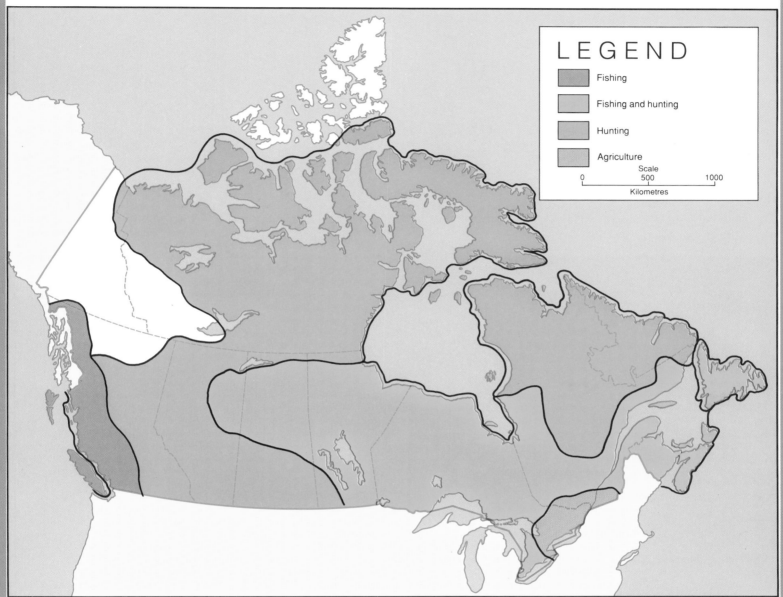

LEGEND

Fishing

Fishing and hunting

Hunting

Agriculture

Scale
0   500   1000
Kilometres

West Coast Indians Returning from the Hunt,
painting by Thomas Mower Martin

A Buffalo Pound, engraving by Edw. Finden

Canada
NATIVE PEOPLES—TODAY

Dakota, Alberta

Cowichan, British Columbia

Where Native Peoples Live

Newfoundland	1.3
Prince Edward Island	0.2
Nova Scotia	2.0
New Brunswick	1.3
Quebec	11.4
Ontario	23.5
Manitoba	12.0
Saskatchewan	10.9
Alberta	14.6
British Columbia	17.8
Yukon	0.7
Northwest Territories	4.3

= 100 %

Cree, Saskatchewan

LEGEND
Major Linguistic Groups

- Algonkian
- Athapascan
- Haida
- Iroquoian
- Kootenayan
- Salishan
- Siouan
- Tlingit
- Tsimshian
- Waskashan
- Inuktituk
- .... Possible boundaries for the proposed new territory Nunavut.

Canadian Native Peoples Population (1990)

	Total Population (Status Indians only)	Number of Bands	Number of Reserves	Area of Reserves km²
Canada	466 337	596	2 242	2 683 454
Atlantic Provinces	18 433	31	68	30 292
Quebec	45 742	39	30	72 273
Ontario	107 862	126	192	712 003
Manitoba	67 092	60	110	221 819
Saskatchewan	72 111	68	147	630 729
Alberta	57 590	42	91	656 865
British Columbia	80 742	196	1 577	342 716
Yukon	5 973	15	25	3 197
Northwest Territories	10 792	19	2	13 562

Micmac, Cape Breton Island, Nova Scotia

Inuit, North West Territories

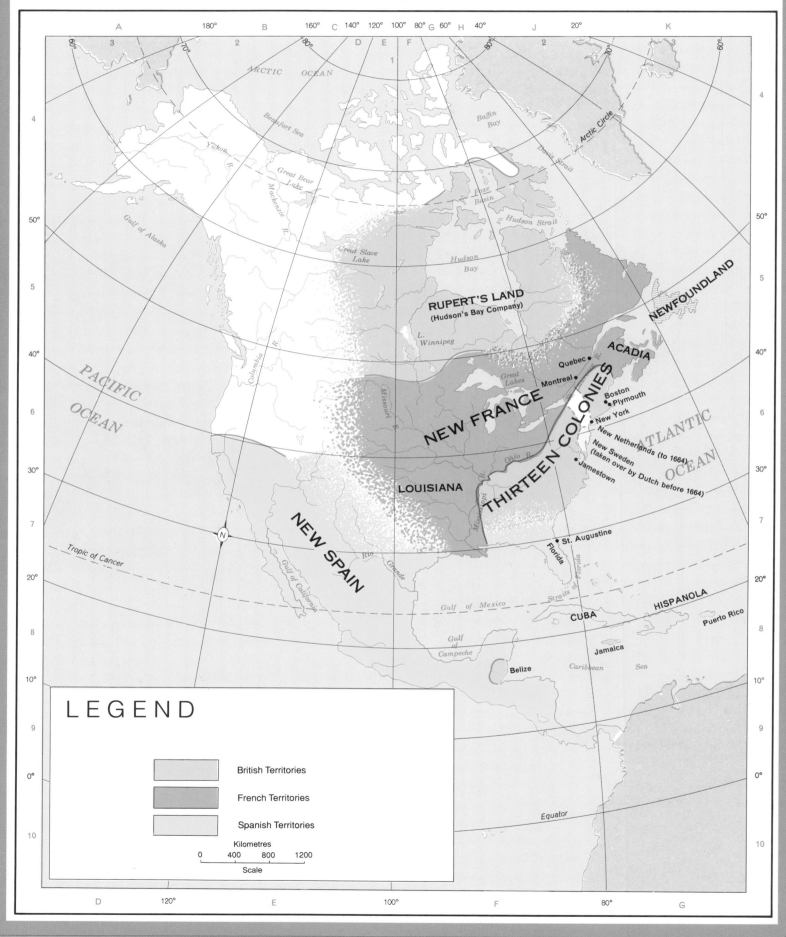

North America
AREAS OF COLONIAL INFLUENCE—1664

ARCTIC OCEAN

Beaufort Sea

Baffin Bay

Arctic Circle

Davis Strait

Yukon R.

Great Bear Lake

Mackenzie R.

Foxe Basin

Hudson Strait

Gulf of Alaska

Great Slave Lake

Hudson Bay

NEWFOUNDLAND

RUPERT'S LAND
(Hudson's Bay Company)

L. Winnipeg

ACADIA

PACIFIC OCEAN

Columbia R.

Missouri R.

Great Lakes

Quebec

Montreal

Boston
Plymouth
New York
New Netherlands (to 1664)
New Sweden
(taken over by Dutch before 1664)

NEW FRANCE

THIRTEEN COLONIES

ATLANTIC OCEAN

Ohio R.

Mississippi R.

LOUISIANA

Jamestown

NEW SPAIN

St. Augustine

Florida

Tropic of Cancer

Gulf of California

Rio Grande

Straits of Florida

Gulf of Mexico

CUBA

HISPANOLA

Puerto Rico

Gulf of Campeche

Jamaica

Belize

Caribbean Sea

Equator

LEGEND

	British Territories
	French Territories
	Spanish Territories

Kilometres

0   400   800   1200

Scale

Canada
POLITICAL DEVELOPMENT

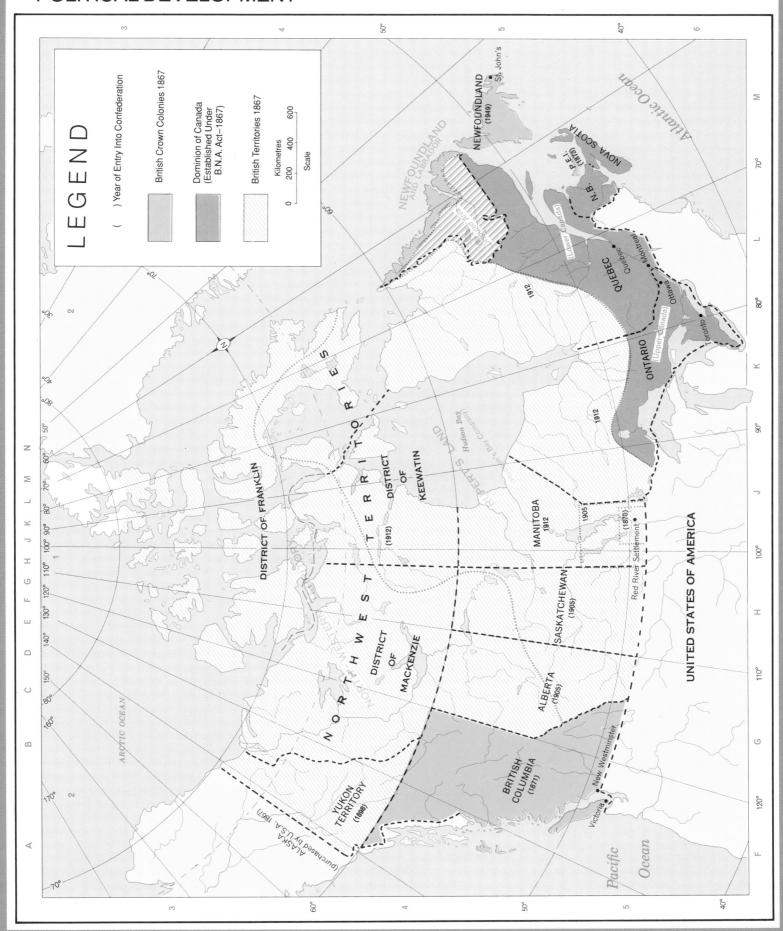

LEGEND

( ) Year of Entry Into Confederation

British Crown Colonies 1867

Dominion of Canada (Established Under B.N.A. Act—1867)

British Territories 1867

Scale

Kilometres

0   200   400   600

ARCTIC OCEAN

Atlantic Ocean

Pacific Ocean

NEWFOUNDLAND AND LABRADOR

NEWFOUNDLAND (1949)

St. John's

NOVA SCOTIA (1867)

P.E.I. (1873)

N.B.

Lower Canada

QUEBEC

Quebec

Montreal

Ottawa

Upper Canada

ONTARIO

Toronto

1912

1912

1912

Hudson Bay

RUPERT'S LAND

(Hudson's Bay Company)

NORTHWEST TERRITORIES

DISTRICT OF FRANKLIN

DISTRICT OF KEEWATIN (1912)

DISTRICT OF MACKENZIE

MANITOBA 1912

1905

MANITOBA (1870)

Red River Settlement

SASKATCHEWAN (1905)

ALBERTA (1905)

BRITISH COLUMBIA (1871)

New Westminster

Victoria

YUKON TERRITORY (1898)

ALASKA (purchased by U.S.A. 1867)

UNITED STATES OF AMERICA

Gazetteer

On the following pages are two alphabetical lists of all the important names that appear on the maps in this atlas. The first list is of Canadian names. The other is of the rest of the world.

Names are generally followed by the name of the country, continent, or ocean in which they are situated. The Canadian names, however, only include the name of the province in which the place is found. Those names that appear more than once are indexed only once.

After each name there is a figure that shows the page number of the map on which you will find the place. Following this is a letter and another figure. These refer to the letters along the top and bottom of each map and to the figures along each side. Together they will help you find the position of any place on the map.

Physical features are also listed in the gazetteer. Each feature is abbreviated, set in italics, and followed by the term indicating its nature. Also, names of countries may appear in an abbreviated form on a map. Some examples appear below and others are shown with underlining on the pages that follow.

Names appearing more than once are listed in this order: first, place names; second, political divisions; and third, physical features.

ABBREVIATIONS

Afghan.	Afghanistan
Ala.	Alabama
Alsk.	Alaska
Alta.	Alberta
Antarc.	Antarctica
arch.	archipelago
Arc. Oc.	Arctic Ocean
Ariz.	Arizona
At. Oc.	Atlantic Ocean
Aust.	Australia
b.	bay
bas.	basin
B.C.	British Columbia
c.	cape
Calif.	California
C.A.R.	Central African Republic
C. Am.	Central America
Can.	Canada
Carib. S.	Caribbean Sea
ch.	channel
Congo Rep.	Congo Republic
Conn.	Connecticut
cur.	current
Cz.	Czech Republic
Dem.	Democratic
Den.	Denmark
des.	desert
dist.	district
Dom. Rep.	Dominican Republic
Eur.	Europe
f.	feature
Fla.	Florida
Fr.	France, French

g.	gulf
G. of Mex.	Gulf of Mexico
Guat.	Guatemala
Hon.	Honduras
i., Is., is.	island(s)
Ill.	Illinois
in.	inlet
Ind. Oc.	Indian Ocean
isth.	isthmus
l., L., ls.	lake(s)
Louis.	Louisiana
Man.	Manitoba
Mass.	Massachusetts
Md.	Maryland
Med. S.	Mediterranean Sea
Mex.	Mexico
Mich.	Michigan
Minn.	Minnesota
Miss.	Mississippi
mt., Mt., mts.	mountain(s)
N.	North, Northern; New
N. Am.	North America
N.B.	New Brunswick
N.C.	North Carolina
N.D.	North Dakota
Neb.	Nebraska
Neth.	Netherlands
Nfld.	Newfoundland
N.H.	New Hampshire
Nic.	Nicaragua
N.J.	New Jersey
N. Mex.	New Mexico
N.S.	Nova Scotia
N.W.T.	Northwest Territories
N.Y.	New York
N.Z.	New Zealand
Okla.	Oklahoma
Ont.	Ontario

Pa.	Pennsylvania
Pac. Oc.	Pacific Ocean
Pak.	Pakistan
P.E.I.	Prince Edward Island
pen.	peninsula
Port.	Portuguese
prov.	province
pt.	point
Que.	Quebec
r.	river
reg.	region
rep., Rep.	republic
res.	reservoir
res. stat.	research station
s., S.	sea, Sea; South
S. Am.	South America
Sask.	Saskatchewan
S.C.	South Carolina
sd.	sound
S.D.	South Dakota
S.I.	Slovak Republic
Sp.	Spain, Spanish
St., Ste.	Saint(e)
str.	strait
S.W.	South West
Switz.	Switzerland
Tas.	Tasmania
Tenn.	Tennessee
terr., Terr.	territory
Tex.	Texas
U.S.A.	United States of America
Venez.	Venezuela
W.	West
Wash.	Washington
W. Virg.	West Virginia
Zimb.	Zimbabwe

THE WORLD (Except Canada)

The World

Ten Largest Countries of the World (by size)

1.	Russia	17 075 272 km²
2.	Canada	9 976 139 km²
3.	China	9 561 000 km²
4.	U.S.A.	9 363 353 km²
5.	Brazil	8 511 965 km²
6.	Australia	7 696 810 km²
7.	India	3 287 580 km²
8.	Argentina	2 766 889 km²
9.	Sudan	2 505 813 km²
10.	Algeria	2 381 741 km²

Earth's Oceans

Atlantic Ocean	26%
Indian Ocean	21%
Arctic Ocean	4%
Pacific Ocean	49%
Total salt water surface 100%	

Ten Longest Rivers

1.	Nile, Africa	6 695 km
2.	Amazon, South America	6 437 km
3.	Chang Jiang, Asia	6 379 km
4.	Mississippi, U.S.A.	6 270 km
5.	Ob-Irtysh, Asia	5 410 km
6.	Huang, Asia	4 672 km
7.	Amur, Asia	4 416 km
8.	Congo, Africa	4 374 km
9.	Lena, Asia	4 400 km
10.	Mackenzie, North America	4 241 km

Ten Largest Lakes/Inland Seas

1.	Caspian Sea, Asia	371 145 km²
2.	Lake Superior, North America	82 135 km²
3.	Lake Victoria, Africa	69 511 km²
4.	Aral Sea, Asia (salt)	64 526 km²
5.	Lake Huron, North America	59 593 km²
6.	Lake Michigan, North America	57 779 km²
7.	Lake Tanganyika, Africa	32 906 km²
8.	Lake Baykal, Asia	31 512 km²
9.	Great Bear Lake, North America	31 341 km²
10.	Nyasa, Africa	28 890 km²

North America

Area: 24 258 000 km²
Highest point: Mt. McKinley   6 194 m
Lowest point: Death Valley   86 m below sea level

South America

Area: 17 823 000 km²
Highest point: Aconcagua   6 960 m
Lowest point: Salinas Grande   40 m below sea level

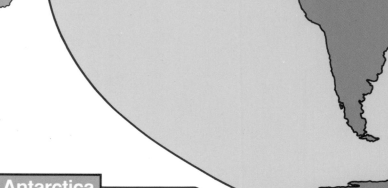

Antarctica

Area: 13 209 500 km²
Highest point: Vinson Massif   5 140 m
Lowest point: Sea level

Ten Notable Deserts

1.	Sahara, Africa	9 000 000 km²
2.	Rub Al Kahli, Asia	650 000 km²
3.	Kalahari, Africa	583 000 km²
4.	Chihuahuan, North America	363 000 km²
5.	Taklimakan, Asia	363 000 km²
6.	Kara Kum, Asia	311 000 km²
7.	Gibson, Australia	310 000 km²
8.	Nubian, Africa	260 000 km²
9.	Syrian, Africa	260 000 km²
10.	Thar, Asia	260 000 km²